Can mountain rescue?

A pocket guide to safety on the hill

Second edition

by Judy Whiteside

FOREWORD BY
HRH PRINCE WILLIAM OF WALES

Call out mountain rescue?

A pocket guide to safety on the hill

Second edition

by Judy Whiteside

**FOREWORD BY
HRH PRINCE WILLIAM OF WALES**

Published by
Mountain Rescue England and Wales
in association with
the British Cave Rescue Council

First published as *Call Out Mountain Rescue* 2008
Second edition published as *Call Out Mountain Rescue?* 2010

Published by Mountain Rescue England and Wales
in association with
the British Cave Rescue Council

Editor: Judy Whiteside
editor@mountain.rescue.org.uk
www.mountain.rescue.org.uk

Mountain Rescue England and Wales is a charitable trust
number 222596.

ISBN: 978-0-9501765-9-8

Front cover image: Avalanche rescue in Patterdale,
February 2010 by Andy McAlea.
Photography elsewhere as credited.
Illustrations and maps by Judy Whiteside.
Lightning Advice by Steve Long.

contents

© Goodyear

iii

What to do in case of emergency

1 ❖ Safeguard the casualty against further fall or injury and ensure you and your party are safe.

2 ❖ Note state of consciousness. If the casualty is unconscious, he or she may start moving vigorously or become violent on regaining consciousness.

3 ❖ Check the airway, breathing and pulse of the casualty and continue to monitor.

4 ❖ Stop any bleeding by pressure with a handkerchief or first aid dressing.

5 ❖ Make the casualty as comfortable as you can. Keep dry, insulate from the ground, moving them as little as possible in the process (especially if there is a possibility of spinal injury) and make warm (extra clothing, survival bag).

6 ❖ Try to attract help by shouting, whistle blasts, torch flashing or use the distress signal. International Distress Signal – Six good long blasts/flashes within 1 minute (Reply – Three blasts/flashes within 1 minute). Keep signalling until help arrives.

7 ❖ Send for help, with a written note of the incident details. Dial 999, ask for POLICE or on the coast ask for COASTGUARD and be ready to give a CHALET report – Casualty details, Hazards, Access, Location, Equipment at the scene, Type of Incident. (See page 27 for more detail).

8 ❖ Stay at the telephone until the police or mountain rescue team make contact. Or stay where your mobile phone is known to be making contact – and leave it switched on.

contents

FOR RESCUE:
DIAL 999 AND ASK FOR THE POLICE
OR ON THE COAST ASK FOR
COASTGUARD

v

© Simon Walton

MOUNTAIN
RESCUE

MOUNTAIN   RESCUE
LAND ROVER
AMBULANCE
MOBILE 2   MOBIL
PE08 TWD

COCKERMOUTH FLOODS
NOVEMBER 2009
Photo:Cockermouth MRT

ST JAMES'S PALACE

foreword

Since 2007, when I became Patron of Mountain Rescue England and Wales, I have been privileged on a number of occasions to witness for myself the extraordinary professionalism of our rescue teams. Most recently, these have come through my training to become a pilot with the Royal Air Force's Search and Rescue Force, which has shown me at first hand how the different elements of the rescue services work so brilliantly together to save lives. The difference between us, though, is that we, in the Royal Air Force, are paid to do the job we do; the Mountain Rescue teams are all volunteers. Their dedication is just amazing, and we owe a huge debt of gratitude to them all.

This latest edition of the handbook imparts advice from Mountain Rescue's wealth of experience which, if followed, could save your life, and the lives of those you are with. I recommend it to you highly, and wish you well in the hills and the mountains.

William

Photo: By kind permission of
Prince William © Hugo Burnand

Why dids't thou
promise such
a beauteous day
And make me
travel forth
without my cloak
To let base
clouds o'ertake
me in my way
Hiding thy
bravery in their
rotten smoke?

William◗
Shakespeare

1

It's late. The sun dips behind a view which, only moments ago, lifted your heart with its breathtaking beauty and the cold air rushes in, chilling your weary bones. Or maybe not. Maybe you're miles from anywhere, it's cold and wet and visibility is down to zero.

Whatever the scenario, you're in trouble. One of your party has had an accident and you need help. Who do you call?

No matter how experienced or careful you are, how well equipped or well prepared, in the blink of an eye you might find yourself – or your companions – in need of rescue. Your life in the hands of a rescue team. And, wherever you walk or climb in the mountains and moorland of England and Wales, there is a rescue team equipped and ready to help. Twenty four hours a day, three hundred and sixty five days a year – come rain, snow or sunshine.

The mountain and cave rescue service in England and Wales is provided free of charge to those who need it, by teams of highly trained individuals who take pride in their voluntary ethic. Rescue team members are, by necessity, competent all-weather mountaineers who undergo rigorous training in search techniques, stretcher handling in a diversity of conditions, communications, advanced first aid and helicopter protocol – whatever it takes to give the casualty their best possible chance of safety, survival and recovery. And often to make the difference between life and death. They are familiar with their local terrain and well versed in the idiosyncrasies of the weather and atmospheric conditions in their own geographical area.

Teams are called through the 999 system to work with the statutory emergency services where their specialist skills, equipment and knowledge are invaluable. Team members also work alongside HM Coastguard, RAF mountain rescue teams, National Park Rangers, RAF and Royal Navy search and rescue helicopters, the Air Ambulance and the RNLI. All these bodies work together at the incident site and in the planning and organisation of a rescue.

The last few years have seen a considerable increase in the number of non-mountain incidents, in more urban based searches for children or elderly, confused or potentially suicidal people missing from home. The specialist knowledge and skills of mountain rescue team members were vital in the immediate aftermath of the Lockerbie disaster and have been called upon during a number of high profile murder enquiries, including the Cumbria shootings in June 2010. Many teams provide cover for their local ambulance service during heavy snow conditions, and others have assisted the fire service in dealing with moorland fires. Team members were first on scene at the Grayrigg rail crash and have attended at several coach crashes. Most people are familiar with the news stories surrounding the heavy flooding in Cumbria during November 2009, when rescue teams from across the north west worked together over several days to rescue people from their homes and businesses, but few are aware of the mountain rescue involvement in the Sheffield floods of 2007.

Taking care in the mountains

Mountains and moorlands can be treacherous places without proper care and there are many, many ways to enjoy the mountain environment.

Should you be unfortunate enough to need our help, you'll receive a professional, world class service. Quite frankly, we'd rather you didn't become just another mountain rescue statistic! But what if you do become involved in an accident? What if you meet an avalanche or a thunderstorm threatens? This book takes you through a few of the 'What ifs?' and shows how you can take a few steps towards taking care of yourself, your companions and the environment. And the bibliography at the back of the book lists further sources of information.

So take to the hills and enjoy!

Long term prep

Develop the mountaineering skills you need to judge potential hazard, including the ability to read a map – both before your trip and on the hoof – what equipment to carry and how to use it, how to assess changes in the weather and when it might be wise to turn back.

Learn the basic principles of first aid – airway, breathing, circulation and the recovery position. It could make the difference between life and death.

Find the right equipment and know how to use it before you set out. The most advanced ice axe in the world is little use if you've never practiced self arrest.

Map stuff

● Loosen up! Remove the stiff outer cover from the map. May not look as pretty but it'll be far easier to fold!
● Fold it up. Before you set off, fold your map as small as possible so just the area you want is visible, then secure it with a couple of rubber bands.

Route planning

It pays to gather as much information as possible about your intended route, and the area in general, from up-to-date maps, guidebooks, local knowledge and weather centres. For information about open access land, check out www.naturalengland.org.uk.

Work out a timescale for your trip, anticipating any possible blackspots such as flooding or avalanche risk, and daylight hours available, then plan your route including potential escape routes to cater for a change in the weather or the condition of your party.

Your party

Think about the equipment, experience, capabilities and enthusiasm of your party members, taking into account the time of year, the terrain and nature of the trip – and choose your routes accordingly.

Each member of the party should be kitted out as an individual but if some are too young or unable to carry even a small rucksack, it may need careful organisation to avoid the 'but I thought you had it' syndrome.

Additional items such as a sleeping bag and, on certain terrain, a hill walking rope could be very useful and make a significant contribution to the self sufficiency of a group. But take care not to overload the individual – heavy rucksacks can considerably slow a party and accelerate the onset of exhaustion. Ultimately, a judgement has to be made, taking account of the make-up of the group, their strengths and weaknesses, the time of year, weather conditions and the nature of your intended route.

There's safety in numbers but, if you prefer to go it alone, be aware of the extra risk and always leave your route plan with a friend or relative.

What to take

● Wear **suitable footwear** with a treaded sole which provide support for the ankles. If the sole is worn, the front edge or the heel cut away, your boots are a potential hazard!

● **Clothing should be colourful, warm, windproof and waterproof** and always carry spare, plus hat and gloves (even in summer when the tops and open moorland can still be bitingly cold and windy). A layering system comprising at least a base layer, mid layer and windproof/waterproof outer shell, designed to wick moisture away from the body, should keep you warm, dry and comfortable. We definitely do not recommend you wear jeans – they offer little protection from the elements and may shrink when cold and wet, wicking vital warmth away from the body.

● **Warm your toes – wear a hat!** Up to 70% of the body heat you lose is lost through areas of exposed skin – the top of your head, your face and hands – so good headgear and gloves are important.

● Take **ample food and drink** for each member of your party, and then some. High energy foods such as chocolate and dried fruit are ideal for a quick hit.

In cold, wet weather a warm drink is advisable, and always carry water – even in cool weather it's easy to become dehydrated. Fluids are vital for the maintenance of body temperature.

Exercise produces sweat which cools the body down as it evaporates. The fluids lost to sweat need replacing to avoid overheating and possible heat exhaustion. As a rule of thumb – if you're thirsty, you are already dehydrated!

● A **map and compass** are essential pieces of kit and should be carried on your person, not in your rucksack – and referred to on a regular basis! Knowing exactly where you are makes all sorts of decisions so much easier, quicker and more accurate.

● Take a **whistle** and learn the signal for rescue. Six good long blasts. Stop for one minute. Repeat. Carry on the whistle blasts until someone reaches you. And don't stop because you've heard a reply – rescuers may be using your blasts as a direction finder, especially in poor visibility.

● A **torch** is an absolute must, with spare batteries and bulbs. In case of difficulties, a torch can be used for signalling, in the same pattern as for whistle blasts.

● At least one **reliable watch** in the party.

● A **mobile phone and GPS** may be useful tools but don't rely on your mobile to get you out of trouble. In many areas of the hills and mountains there is no signal coverage.

● Climbers and mountain bikers should wear a **helmet**. In winter conditions an **ice axe, crampons and survival bag** are essential.

taking care

What to take with you

Taking care in the mountains

8

Packin' the sack:1

Summer

- Rucksack
- Food and drink for the day
- Whistle
- Watch
- Map and compass
- Torch
- Boots/trainers
- Socks
- Trousers/shorts
- Base layer
- Mid layer
- Outer layer
- Sunglasses

And just in case...

- Waterproof overtrousers
- Waterproof jacket
- Hat
- Gloves
- Spare clothing
- Pen and paper
- First aid kit/sunscreen
- Survival bag

- Rucksack
- Food and drink for the day
- Whistle
- Watch
- Map and compass
- Torch
- Boots (possibly crampons)
- Socks
- Trousers
- Base layer
- Mid layer
- Outer layer
- Waterproof overtrousers
- Waterproof jacket
- Hat and scarf
- Gloves/overmitts
- Gaiters
- Thermarest mat

And just in case...

- Sunglasses
- Goggles
- Spare clothing
- Pen and paper
- First aid kit/sunscreen
- Survival bag

Winter

● Basic **first aid kit** comprising any essential medication (eg. for diabetes, asthma, angina, allergies), scissors, penknife, plasters/blister gel pads, paracetamol, safety pins, antihistamine, insect repellent, sting/bite relief, sunscreen, antiseptic sachet, wet wipes, tissues.

● Emergency **survival kit** comprising spare clothing for warmth and lightweight bothy bag – a potential life saver if you are benighted or injured. Carry spare specs or contact lenses if you wear them, make sure you have a couple of watches in the party, and always pack some paper (preferably waterproof) and a pencil.

Make a note

In the event of an accident, the mountain rescue team will want as much information as possible about the incident, the terrain, any casualties and possible injuries. On waterproof paper, make out a couple of 'casualty cards' before your trip – see page 26 for the sort of details you may require. Keep in the rucksack – along with a chinagraph pencil – and they'll act as a handy aide memoire when you need them.

Pack the rucksack – basic kit for summer and winter

Taking care in the mountains

10

Packin' the sack: 2

You might well delight in finding that twelve month old Mars bar flattened at the bottom of the sack but it's worthwhile having a sort out and kit review every couple of outings at least!

Think about your trip. What do you really need to carry? We've given you some basic guidelines on page 9 but, now you've decided what to take, pack with care. Get the weight balance wrong and, not only will you tire more easily, you could be storing up problems for your knees, hips, back and neck.

● First off, think about lining the whole sack with a bin liner – even if you have a waterproof outer cover. No point having spare clothing if it's damp and cold!

● If you carry a stove and fuel, wrap in a well sealed polythene bag and keep in a separate pocket – well away from your lunch.

● Heavy stuff should sit as close to your lower back (centre of gravity) as possible, lighter stuff towards the outside. Take care to spread the balance across the width of the rucksack and avoid sharp edges and corners against your back.

● Pack the stuff you need to access frequently on the top or inside pockets – food, water, basic first aid kit, suncream.

● Don't have things dangling from the outside of the rucksack.

● If you carry poles, be aware that an upward pointing pole, strapped to the side of the rucksack may act as a handy lightning conductor!

Before you set off

- **Charge your mobile** phone battery!

- **Check the weather** forecast and local conditions before you leave. Mountains can be major undertakings and, in the winter months especially, night falls early.

There's a huge amount of data and advice freely available to anyone setting out on the hill – national and regional TV and radio, online weather forecasts, local information boards, telephone data. Take note of the information available, not just for safety reasons, but for comfort and viability. There can't be many reasons why you'd want to walk into the teeth of a cold wind when you could reverse your route and have the elements working with you!

- **Eat well** before you start out – cereals and carbohydrates release energy slowly throughout the day.

- **Leave your route plan** – including start and finishing points, estimated time of return and contact details – with an appropriate party (home, hotel, camp site), in case of emergency, and always report your return. If your plans change for any reason – navigation error, weather conditions, your trip takes longer than anticipated – let the relevant people know so the emergency services are not activated in good faith where no problem exists. And do it at the first opportunity – not after the pubs shut!

* Stop thief!

Avoid leaving details of your intended route on display in the car. It could lead to false alarm through inaccurate information and even theft.

On the hill

● **Keep an eye on the weather** throughout the day and note your location related to the map in case visibility deteriorates suddenly.

● **Keep together**. Allow the slowest in the party to determine the pace. Don't be tempted to allow two or three to fall behind, or stop for lunch and 'catch up later'. Make sure everyone knows the route and that each member of the party carries a map and compass. Take special care of the youngest and weakest in dangerous places.

It's easier to lose someone on the hill than you think. Often it's the extremes of a party who suffer – the weakest, least knowledgeable and most poorly equipped get left behind or the keenest and fittest dash ahead, get lost and fall off trying to descend. Stay together and it isn't a problem.

● **Watch for signs of hypothermia** particularly in bad weather – disorientation, shivering, tiredness, pale complexion and loss of circulation in hands or toes, discarding of vital clothing. Children and older people are especially susceptible. And be aware that members of your own party may become hypothermic if stopped by someone else's accident. See 'Hypothermia' on page 28 for more detail.

● **Don't press on** if conditions turn against you. It's no disgrace to turn back even if this upsets a long planned adventure, however disappointing. Remember, a party must be governed by its weakest member.

Rock climbing

This sport takes people into many different environments – sea cliffs, slate quarries, roadside crags, high mountain crags – posing interesting dilemmas about what kind of kit to take. For example, on a low sea cliff traverse, should a climber take a rope or a life jacket? Different environments bring different hazards but here's a few simple guidelines:–

● **Wearing a helmet** could save your life. The majority of serious injuries are to the head (the one area of the body least able to withstand them) whether from a fall, falling rock or debris dislodged by the climber above. A helmet could mean the difference between life and death.

● **Take care on the scramble** to or from a climb. Lack of concentration – be it due to

14

Dangers you can avoid

- Precipices.
- Slopes of ice or steep snow.
- Very steep grass slopes, especially if frozen or wet.
- Unstable boulders.
- Gullies, gorges and stream beds.
- Streams in spate.
- Snow cornices on ridges or gully tops.
- Exceeding your experience and abilities.
- Loss of concentration – especially towards the end of the day.

- Weather changes – mist, gale, rain and snow may be sudden and more extreme than forecast. Watch the sky!
- Ice on path (know how to use an ice axe and crampons).
- Excessive cold or heat (dress appropriately and carry spare clothing).
- Exhaustion (know the signs, rest and keep warm).
- Accident or illness (don't panic – if you send for help, make sure you stay put and the rescuers know exactly where to come).
- Passage of time – especially true when under pressure – allow extra time in winter or night time conditions.
- Over ambition.

Dangers you need to monitor

eageness before or tiredness after – leads to accidents. As does inappropriate footwear – smooth soled friction boots are great on rock but more like skis on grass.

● **Know how to use it!** A rucksack packed with shiny gizmos is only half the story. Whatever equipment you use – from harnesses, ropes, and belay systems, ice axe and crampons, through to GPS and mobile phone technology – the skills to use them correctly are essential and easy to develop.

● **Check tide times** and height if climbing on sea cliffs. A difference of 0.75 metres can substantially alter a route. Weather conditions also influence sea state and swell and can change the nature of routes elsewhere.

● **Check out the nearest landline telephone** just in case – before you hit a problem!

● **Take account of other people** who may be climbing in the same area. That stone you knocked off by accident may not be a danger to you, but who is below? Everyone is there to have a good day's climbing and consideration of factors like noise, leading through etc, can only add to the experience.

Dangers you can avoid

Dangers you need to monitor

Taking care in the mountains

...and more map stuff

- Cut it up. Yes we felt you wince, but there is often a lot on the map that you will never use for hill navigation. So why not trim it down to cover just the areas you want, incorporating grid refs and the map key, then write the map name in a corner.

- Scribble on it. Mark a laminated map with chinagraph pencil to plot features as you get to them and make relocation easier. Double top tip – these can be removed later with toothpaste!

Find your way around

Okay so we've recommended you learn the basic skills before you set off into the hills. How? Well, you could check out your nearest mountaineering instructor at www.ami.org.uk, or look for courses at the national climbing centres at Plas y Brenin in North Wales and Glenmore Lodge in Scotland. And there's a wealth of informative books out there – we've listed a few at the back of the book.

In the meantime, what we do know is that poor navigation is often a significant factor in mountain rescue incidents, so here's a few tips to help you on your way.

- **Picture the scene** – before setting off, trace a finger across your planned route, build a picture, and talk it through to yourself, like a video clip. 'Past a wooded bit, church on the left, alongside the stream then up a steep bit to a wall...' It'll be easier to remember when you're on the hill and may ring a few bells if you go wrong.

Keep watching – once you're on your way, carry on adding to that mental picture, noting any distinguishing features and using them to orient yourself on the map.

How far, how fast? As a rule, you will walk at 4km an hour, or 1km every 15 minutes. Which translates as 1cm every 15 minutes on a 1:25,000 map. And bear in mind that walking uphill is likely to slow you down, so add a minute for every 10m climbed.

Don't get complacent, stuff the map in the sack and forget about it. If you do go wrong, you'll notice sooner and it will be easier to retrace your steps if you've kept an eye on things.

Keep it short – navigate in short sections of about 500 metres. Stop, take stock of the surroundings, check the map then carry on towards your next point.

Collect stuff – if you're worried about missing a particular path or junction, pinpoint a collecting feature just beyond what you're looking for and walk towards that. If you reach it, you'll know you've passed the bit you were actually aiming for and can retrack.

Don't panic! If it doesn't seem to be working out, take a few moments to recheck your navigation and don't be afraid to retrace your steps.

Navigation tips – finding your way around

Taking care in the mountains

Maximise your mobile

Your mobile phone may not be the most reliable way of calling for help. Batteries can very quickly run flat and signal coverage in the hills is still a hit and miss affair. That said, the use of mobiles has grown enormously in the last ten years and the majority of calls for mountain rescue help are made by mobile. The days of running down the hill to the nearest telephone box to summon help – it would appear – are well and truly over.

So, how do you make the most of your mobile phone and maximise your chances of maintaining contact once you've called for help?

● **Keep your mobile in a plastic bag** somewhere warm and accessible, where you can hear it in the prevailing conditions. And, if possible, pack a spare battery in a separate plastic bag.

● **If the signal is poor, stand still!** Keep the phone in one position to maintain the connection.

● **Shelter the microphone** from the wind and increase the receive volume settings as necessary.

● **Fully charge the battery** (and the spare!) before setting off.

● **Minimise your call time** to conserve battery power.

● **Schedule your point of contact calls** and switch off by arrangement when not required.

● The police or coastguard may establish a calling schedule with you – for example, every 20 minutes or so – between which you may arrange to turn off your mobile phone.

● **Check for coverage with every phone in the party**. Use one phone at a time to preserve batteries – or swap batteries.

● If there's only one phone and it shows no coverage, disconnect the battery for one minute and reconnect. Switch on and try again.

● **Consider taking all the available phones to a more prominent location** to get network coverage. Take care not to get lost in the process and remember that **sometimes a ten minute walk up the hill is sufficient to get you a signal, rather than running down the valley for an hour.**

● If you cannot move and/or have insufficient network coverage to make a voice call, **try sending a text message** from all the available mobile phones in your party, to your point of contact.

● In many mountain areas, the **deaf, hearing and speech impaired** can now send an emergency 999 text message to a dedicated number. Refer to the appropriate police authority for more details – before you set out!

Maximising use of your mobile phone

Taking care in the mountains

21 ●◆ CUILLIN RIDGE. THE ISLE OF SKYE
Photo: Stuart Roy

Mountaineering in Scotland

Conditions in Scotland are materially different from those in England and Wales. The country is more rugged, the walk-ins can be considerably further, and inhabited dwellings in mountainous areas are few and far between.

If your experience is only of walking and climbing in England and Wales you may be unprepared – mentally and physically, and in the equipment you carry – for the often unreliable and more severe conditions north of the border. Even in summer, blizzards of snow or sleet can occur above 2500 feet and, in winter, the snowstorms may reach Arctic severity. Gale force winds are frequent and increase exhaustion both by the general buffeting and disturbance of balance and by their chilling effect on the body temperature.

Mountaineering in Scotland demands a high standard of physical fitness and endurance, some experience of snow conditions, adequate reserves of food, warm and windproof clothing,

Pack the zapper!

The Scottish midge is renowned. Between May and September it's a prolific pest and it's after your blood. So pack the insect repellent and be prepared!

Mountaineering in Scotland

Taking care in the mountains

Midges

Of the 1,000 plus species of midge in the world, about forty live in Scotland and 90% of the biting attacks on humans and animals are down to a single species – Culicoides Impunctatus or Meanbh-chuileag in Gaelic, meaning 'tiny fly'.

In Scotland, there are two generations of midges between May and September, producing an estimated ten midges per man, woman and child in the entire country – and that's before the tourists arrive!

They thrive in habitats rich in organic matter such as peat bogs, creating havoc with walkers, and target their victims by sensing carbon dioxide in exhaled breath and by smell.

If you're in forgiving mood though, it's not all bad news – the little beggars do play their part in the bigger ecological picture. The adult midge helps to feed some species of bat and bird and the larvae do help break down decaying organic matter. Just as well as a single female may lay more than 200 eggs in her lifetime.

Check out **www.midgeforecast.co.uk** before you travel north. The site categorises five 'midge levels' from the basic Level 1 (Negligible) through to Level 5 (Nuisance), in seven day forecasts for 38 areas across Scotland. Their 'Smidge Forecast' app, available for iPhone, uses Google Maps to indicate where the midges are at their worst. And you can also contribute to the Midge Map by tweeting back midge readings – the app uses geolocation to locate your exact position and lists your reading.

an ice axe and appropriate boots. In winter, boots with Vibram soles and crampons, for use on hard snow and ice, are a sensible combination. Vibram soles without crampons on snow and ice are useless.

Winter days are short, so expeditions should start early, if necessary before dawn. During the day, keep a careful watch on the weather and snow conditions and, if there is any doubt about the suitability of the surface, the weather and the ability of the party to complete the expedition before dark, remember that retreat is better than benightment or the need for a rescue party.

Beware the biting beasties!

- **Keep skin covered.** In fact, think about investing in a midge hood. Made from very fine mesh it will protect your face and scalp from those dreaded itchy lumps.
- **Wear light coloured clothing** – dark colours are more attractive to biting insects.
- **Remember midges and mozzies are more active at dusk and dawn** so be prepared. Wear a good repellent and reapply regularly.

Mountaineering in Scotland

Bug alert! Midges at large!

Taking care in the mountains

25

In the **event of a mountain incident...**

Dial 999
and ask for the **POLICE**
then **Mountain Rescue**

Be ready to give a **CHALET** report:—

C – Casualties – number, names (and, if possible, age);
type of injuries, for example, lower leg, head injury,
collapse, drowning etc.

H – Hazards to the rescuers – for example, strong winds,
avalanche, rock fall, dangerous animals.

A – Access – the name of mountain area and description of
the terrain. It may be appropriate to describe the approach
and any distinguishing features such as an orange survival
bag. Information on the weather conditions at the incident
site is useful, particularly if you are in cloud or mist.

L – Location of the incident – a grid reference and a
description is ideal. Don't forget to give the map sheet
number and please say if the grid reference is from a GPS
device.

E – Equipment at the scene – for example, torches, other
mobile phones, group shelters, medical personnel.

T – Type of incident – mountain, aircraft, train, etc. Be
prepared to give a brief description of the time and
apparent cause of the incident.

What you can do if... there's an accident

If you have a serious problem, are involved in or witness an accident, take time to assess the seriousness of the situation first. You may be able to help yourselves, there may be steps you can take to make the job of mountain rescue easier and you will be better equipped to provide valuable detail to the emergency services control room.

Assess your options

● Descend to safety?

What will the terrain be like? How far is it to safety? Do you need to support or carry the casualty? Will the casualty's injuries be made worse by movement?

● Find shelter?

Don't use up valuable time and energy unless you are absolutely sure of finding shelter.

● Stay put?

Will the situation be resolved if you stay where you are? If you were moving before the accident, the chances are that you, the casualty and any other members of the party are probably now getting cold. Use your spare clothing and survival bags and take occasional drinks and food to keep the body's systems ticking over. However, do not give the casualty any food or drink before their injuries have been properly assessed.

If you decide to call for mountain rescue, stay exactly where you are. If you are making the call for help, stay by the phone, or at an agreed rendezvous point, until the rescue team has spoken to you. Monitor the casualty's condition at regular intervals, if possible keeping a written record – description of the injuries, the exact location, the time of the accident and, if known, the casualty's name and address – to pass on when help arrives.

● Send for help?

If you decide you need the help of the emergency services, consider whether you need an ambulance or a mountain rescue team. If you are on a driveable road, an ambulance is most appropriate. However, if the injured person is unable to walk or on dangerous terrain, you may need a stretcher and a mountain rescue team.

Dial 999 and ask for the police. The police will then notify the appropriate mountain rescue team who will assess how best to evacuate the casualty as efficiently as possible from the scene of an accident.

What to do
in case of
emergency

Step one:
Check for danger

Step two:
Check for response

Unresponsive?

**Step three:
Call 999, ask for the
Police and then
Mountain Rescue**

Step four:
Open airway

Step 5: Check
for normal breathing

Not breathing normally?

Step six: Start CPR

**30 chest compressions
+ 2 rescue breaths
Repeat until help arrives**

What you can do... while you wait for the rescue team

Okay, so one of your party is injured or feeling unwell. You've dialled 999, called for mountain rescue. A team is on the way. Depending on your location, it may take some time for them to reach you.

How do you deal with a life-threatening situation or prevent an injury being worsened?

From the moment you realise someone is injured, you can take action to help, in six simple steps.

- **Check for danger**
- **Check for response**
- **Call for help**
- **Open the airway**
- **Check for normal breathing**
- **If necessary, start CPR**

What to do in case of emergency

Step one: Check for danger

Is there any further danger? Remember, your first priority is your own safety! Get to the casualty as quickly as possible, without putting yourself or others at risk.

If possible, the casualty should be treated where found. Do not move him any more than is absolutely necessary, unless he is in danger of falling further, or he is in the path of a rock fall.

Step two: Check for response

Is he conscious? A conscious casualty is unlikely to have breathing problems unless there is a chest or facial injury.

If he appears to be unconscious, check for a response. Gently shake his shoulders and ask loudly, 'Hello. Can you hear me? Are you all right?'

If he responds – leave him in the position you found him, provided there is no further danger. Find out what his injuries are and call for mountain rescue if necessary. Continue to reassess his state of consciousness regularly.

Is his heart beating? Taking the casualty's wrist, place your first three fingers just below the crease where his hand and wrist meet, just under the thumb, and press until you can feel the radial pulse.

Step three: Call for help or try to attract attention

If he does not respond, call for help or try to attract attention by shouting, whistle blasts or torch flashing. There may be other walkers and climbers in the area who can assist. Do not leave the casualty at this stage. If you have a mobile signal, dial 999, ask for 'Police' and then 'Mountain Rescue'. Be prepared to give details of the casualty and his injuries, and your location.

Step four: Open the airway

The airway must be open and clear so that air can pass to the lungs – check the casualty's mouth and remove any obstruction such as false teeth, toffees or pooled saliva.

In an unconscious casualty, the tongue may fall backwards, blocking his windpipe. Tilting the head back and lifting the chin forward will help draw the tongue away from the back of the throat.

To open the airway, turn the casualty onto his back. Place one hand on his forehead and two fingers under the chin, then gently tilt his head back and lift his chin.

What to do in case of emergency

32

Step five: Check for normal breathing

● Keeping the airway open, put your ear near his mouth to listen, feel and look for signs of his breathing. Listen for the sounds of breathing, feel the breathe on your cheek, look at his chest for signs of movement. Do this for no more than ten seconds.

Step six: Start CPR

Okay, so he's stopped breathing... If you have any doubt whether his breathing is normal, continue as though it is not normal. If you've never been trained in CPR, don't panic – delivering 'hands-only' CPR might save his life.

Chest compressions

● Kneel alongside the casualty.

● Put the heel of one hand directly on the centre of his chest, between the nipples. Put the heel of the other hand on top, with the fingers interlaced.

● With arms straight, rock forward and push down about 1.5 inches. Avoid putting pressure on the lower part of the breastbone, or the upper abdomen.

● After each compression release all the pressure on the chest, without letting your hands bounce. Repeat the compressions at a rate of 100 per minute.

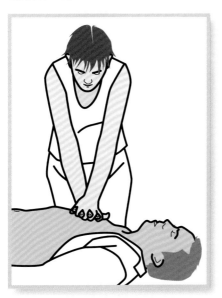

What to do
in case of
emergency

Rescue breaths

● **After 30 compressions** re-check that the casualty's airway is open using the head tilt and chin lift.

● Pinch his nostrils so that air cannot pass through them.

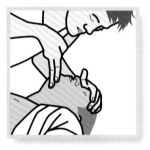

● Take a normal breath then place your mouth around his open mouth so there is no gap through which air can escape.

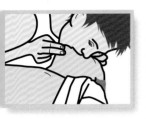

● Blow steadily into the casualty's mouth. You should be able to see his chest rise as you blow into him. Take about one second to make his chest rise as in normal breathing.

● Maintaining head tilt and chin lift, move your mouth away from his and watch for his chest to fall as the air comes out.

● Take another breath and blow into the casualty's mouth once more.

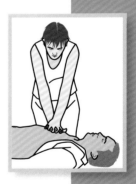

After two rescue breaths immediately return to the correct position to deliver a further 30 chest compressions.

Keep going until the rescue team arrives, or the casualty begins breathing normally. But be warned – this is very tiring! If there are other people giving assistance, take turns to deliver CPR, swapping over every two minutes.

Note: If an unconscious casualty recovers consciousness, he should not be allowed to walk off the hill because he may become dizzy and fall.

What to do in case of emergency

Conscious or not, the casualty is likely to have other injuries

Is he bleeding? If the casualty has fallen, he may be bleeding. Most small cuts will stop in two or three minutes. Larger wounds may continue to lose blood – particularly in a head wound – and movement also leads to continued bleeding.

What you can do...

● To stop bleeding, make a pad from spare cloth such as a handkerchief and press it firmly into the wound. You should maintain **continuous** pressure for at least ten minutes. Use another item, perhaps a scarf or spare shirt, to bind the pad firmly in position so the bleeding is controlled.

● Try to elevate the wound as high as possible above the level of the heart.

Is he comfortable? Keep the casualty dry and insulated from the ground, moving him as little as necessary in the process and use extra clothing or survival blankets to keep him warm.

Are there any other injuries? You've checked for consciousness, noted any cuts and bruises, now check for other injuries. Some will, perhaps, be more obvious than others. That said, most conscious casualties will be able to relate exactly what happened and what they have injured.

Head injuries

Head injuries are common in mountain accidents. Even an apparently 'minor head injury' should be treated with caution.

Feel at the nose, cheekbones, around the contours of the skull and especially the lower jaw for any swelling or obviously abnormal shape.

What you can do...

● To control bleeding from a scalp wound you may have to exert direct pressure on the edges of the wound until the rescue team arrives.

● Do not try to stop bleeding from the ear.

● Stop nasal bleeding by pinching the nose for five minutes.

● Preserve any dislodged teeth in milk or damp tissue.

Note: Remember, a head injury does not cause shock. If the casualty is shocked, another injury is present.

Chest injuries

The most likely cause of chest injury is a substantial fall from height, or direct blow to the chest, resulting in multiple rib fractures or a penetrating wound of the chest wall, for example, from a fall onto an ice axe.

What you can do...

If the casualty is awake, he is likely to be in a lot of pain and may have difficulty breathing.

If he is pink, and able to talk without breathing difficulty, it is unlikely there is any serious chest injury present.

- Put him into a position that makes breathing easiest – usually a sitting position.

With a penetrating chest wound, the casualty is likely to be in extreme pain and shock, and struggling to breathe. The lung on the side of the injury may have collapsed.

- Seal the hole in the chest wall by placing a flattened plastic bag over the hole, using sticking plaster or tape to hold it firmly in place.

- You could encourage the casualty to lie on, or lean towards the injured side, with his head and shoulders supported but he may prefer to be sitting, to improve breathing capacity.

If you don't have a plastic bag or sticky tape, wet the palm of your hand, place it firmly over the hole and keep it there until the rescue team arrives.

Abdominal injuries

The majority of abdominal injuries are 'closed'. A penetrating wound to the abdomen doesn't necessarily indicate damage to the internal organs, but assume the worst as you decide what action to take. There may be little evidence of injury and little or no pain.

What you can do...

● **If you suspect internal injury** all you can do is lie the casualty down, make him as comfortable as possible, insulate him from the ground, protect him from wind-chill and wait for the rescue team.

● **If there is a penetrating wound** treat as above, but cover the wound with a dressing of some sort – a plastic bag or clean cloth.

● **If you see gut protruding from a wound** don't try to push it back in! Ideally, the protruding gut should be covered with a warm, damp, sterile cloth – which is unlikely to be available. A plastic bag is the next best thing.

Spinal injuries

If you suspect a spinal injury – including the bones in the neck – only move the casualty as much as is absolutely necessary for safety and comfort.

The nature of the accident, whether he has fallen even a small distance, and onto what terrain, his position and level of consciousness all give clues to the possibility of spinal injury.

If he can still move his fingers and toes and has normal sensation, the spinal cord is intact but may be unstable. If you are in any doubt, assume injury exists.

What you can do...

Support the casualty's head by placing one hand on either side to limit movement. Maintain this position until the rescue team arrives.

If the casualty has to be rolled into the recovery position, the ideal would be for at least five people to do this, with one person continuing to support his head as described. Avoid bending his spine forwards, (particularly forwards), backwards or sideways.

See pages 51/52 for a step-by-step account of the recovery position.

Limb injuries

If the casualty's arm or leg appears displaced or distorted, or he is unable to use it normally, it may be broken, or there may be major tissue damage. If a conscious casualty can move arms and legs fully, it is unlikely any significant injury exists. Sometimes, the broken bone may protrude through the skin but, more commonly, a break may not be so obvious.

Check for the less obvious injuries...

Upper limbs – press on the collar bones to see if this causes pain. Now squeeze the shoulders gently but firmly and see if this causes pain, or perhaps a moan or some sign of discomfort in the unconscious casualty.

Repeat this process, moving down the upper limbs methodically. Squeeze the upper arms, then the elbows, then the forearms, then the wrists, the hands and, finally, the fingers.

If you find a tender spot in a limb that cannot be used properly, suspect a broken bone in that spot. If there is gross deformity of the shoulder, or of the elbow joint, suspect a dislocation.

Lower limbs – place one hand on the bone just above the right hip and the other hand on the bone just above the left hip. Now, try to bring the hands together. If this action causes pain, suspect a broken pelvis.

Now squeeze your way down the lower limbs as you did with the upper limbs, noting any particularly tender spot in a lower limb which the casualty cannot use properly. In this event, suspect a broken bone.

What you can do...

Your aim is to prevent movement at the place where the bone is broken. Movement causes pain, and pain increases shock. Preventing movement reduces pain, which reduces the degree of shock.

● If a broken bone protrudes through the skin, do not push it back but cover it with a dressing, plastic bag or clean material.

● With **upper limb** injuries, including collar bone and shoulder injuries, the casualty will probably already be holding the injured limb in the position he finds most comfortable (close to the body with the elbow near to a right angle).

● Use a spare piece of clothing as padding between the arm and the body, then bind the limb firmly to the body, including the hand – especially if there is a suspected break at the wrist, forearm or elbow.

● For **lower limb** injuries, use spare clothing to pad between the limbs, particularly between the knees and ankles, then bind the two limbs firmly together.

● If there is a foot or ankle injury, unlace the boot on the foot, then bind the boots together to prevent the feet from rolling sideways and rotating the broken bones.

● Now wait for the rescue team.

Shock

Shock indicates that something is seriously wrong, such as a broken femur, internal injury or severe blood loss. That said, it may be difficult to detect in the early stages as the body compensates. Symptoms to look for include cold, clammy and pale skin, a weak, rapid pulse, thirst, anxiety and confusion or aggression, followed by drowsiness and loss of consciousness.

The rescue team will treat shock as a high priority for rapid evacuation from the hill. For your part, remain calm and stay with the casualty.

What you can do...

● Do not give him anything to eat or drink.

● Keep checking his breathing and level of consciousness while you wait for the rescue team to arrive and make a note of the times when you've done so.

What to do
in case of
emergency

Illnesses

Medical conditions and illness can strike as easily in the mountains as the high street.

What you can do...

● If a member of your party is taken ill and unable to walk off the hill, check first whether he has any medication with him which might help.

● Make him as comfortable as possible, keep him warm, protect him from the wind, insulate from the ground and cold rocks, then send for the rescue team.

Near drowning

Many casualties, particularly children, have survived immersion in cold water for long periods. If you witness a near drowning, it is essential to get the casualty out of the water before attempting CPR.

What you can do...

● Current thinking is that attempts to 'empty water from the lungs' are not effective.

● Open and clear the casualty's airway as described, and commence CPR.

Frostbite

If not treated promptly and effectively, frostbite may lead to the death of tissue – the nose, fingers and toes are particularly susceptible. The only symptom may be a numbness in the affected area.

Pain only occurs with rewarming and may be severe. Frostbitten areas will usually appear white and totally insensitive.

What you can do...

● The most important step is to prevent damage to the sensitive parts. Cover with a non-adherent material such as a plastic bag.

● You should only attempt to rewarm toes, fingers etc when there is no chance of them refreezing – this will most likely be off the hill.

● Rubbing is not an acceptable means of rewarming. In fact, it can actually damage the affected tissue.

Hypothermia

Hypothermia occurs when the body's heat loss exceeds its heat generation. It can develop quickly, even in relatively 'warm' weather, aided and abetted by a number of factors including increased activity, tiredness and dehydration.

The best advice is to avoid hypothermia in the first place with effective clothing, appropriate to the activity, environment and prevailing weather conditions, and by avoiding exhaustion.

The most efficient way to generate heat is through muscular exercise. Eat carbohydrate snacks and take regular drinks. And remember that alcohol, even the night before, can significantly reduce your exercise endurance.

Initially, the hypothermic casualty feels very cold, miserable and disinterested. His skin feels cold under his clothing. Impaired muscle coordination makes him clumsy and stumbling – often falling behind the rest of the party. In most cases, shivering increases as his body works hard to lift body temperature, and then ceases, although a small percentage of people will not shiver at all.

As the hypothermia progresses he becomes increasingly irritable and confused, likely to make serious errors of judgement, and his vision becomes blurred. Confusion eventually gives way to loss of consciousness.

What you can do...

It is not possible to rewarm severely hypothermic casualties on the hill. All your efforts should be directed towards preventing further heat loss.

● In the early stages of hypothermia, an extra layer of windproof clothing, a warm drink and snack, and moving to a more sheltered location may be all that is needed for recovery.

● An unconscious casualty is more difficult to manage because rough handling can trigger cardiac arrest so do not attempt CPR. Shelter and insulate him as best you can, without disturbing his position too much, to prevent further heat loss and wait for the rescue team to arrive.

● It may not be possible to determine whether the casualty is alive or dead whilst still on the hill – however cold they may appear, you should assume they are alive.

We're having a heatwave...

Just as getting cold can have serious consequences, so can getting too hot. We may not be blessed with too many heatwaves on these shores, but when they strike, they can be killers. People with underlying health problems – for example, heart, respiratory or diabetes – are more at risk, as are babies and young children. Some prescription medicines may reduce your tolerance to heat, and physical exercise can increase the risk of heat related illness.

Danger signs to watch for during hot weather include feeling faint or dizzy, breathlessness, vomiting or mild confusion.

What you can do...

● The best advice is to avoid overheating in the first instance. That said, if you've planned a big day on the hill, it may not be possible to avoid exposure to the sun during the hottest part of the day – between 11.00am and 3.00pm – and there may be little shade.

And strenuous activity is the nature of the beast!

Splash out: keep cool!

Loosely tie a damp cotton scarf round your neck, or splash your face and the back of your neck with cold water from time to time to keep the temperature down.

19

top tip

Talc and socks

Long day on the hill? Pack a spare pair of socks and a small pot of talcum powder in the rucksack. A half-time dusting of talc followed by fresh socks works wonders for hot, tired feet!

● Wear a hat, and light loose-fitting clothes designed to wick the sweat away from your skin and keep you cool.

● Drink regularly even if you don't feel thirsty. Have plenty of cold drinks – water or fruit juice – but avoid excess alcohol, caffeine and hot drinks.

If a member of your party appears to be suffering from heat related symptoms...

● Move the casualty to a cooler place if possible, sheltered from the sun.

● Cool them down as quickly as possible by loosening their clothes, sprinkling them with cold water or placing a cool, damp cloth on the back of their neck.

● If they are conscious, give them water or fruit juice to drink.

● Do not give them aspirin or paracetamol as this can make them worse.

What to do in case of emergency

50

Adder bites

Adders often appear in warmer weather. Bites are rare and almost always the result of people handling the snake. The risk of death or serious illness is negligible but there may be considerable pain and swelling. Adders have a limited gape and can only bite fingers or toes in adults – the typical bite producing two puncture marks.

What you can do...

● Snake bites often produce disproportionate anxiety in the victim so reassurance is key. Tourniquets, incisions and the sucking of wounds are strictly for the movies! Immobilise the limb and consider whether the casualty can walk off the hill.

● A visit to hospital is essential as anti-venom may help to control the pain and swelling.

Recovery position

An unconscious casualty who is breathing – injuries and location permitting – should be placed in the recovery position. This allows the tongue to fall forwards, keeping the airway clear.

Step one:

Kneel alongside the casualty. Straighten his legs. Move the arm nearest to you so it is at right angles to his body, elbow bent with the palm of his hand facing up.

Step two:

Bring his other arm towards you, and across his chest. Hold the back of his hand against the casualty's cheek nearest to you.

Step three:

With your other hand, grasp the casualty's far leg, pulling it up to bend at the knee, keeping the foot flat on the ground. Keeping his hand pressed to his cheek, pull on his thigh to roll the casualty onto his side towards you.

Step four:

Adjust the position of his upper leg so hip and knee are bent at right angles to prevent him rolling over onto his face.

Step five:

Tilt the casualty's head back to ensure the airway remains open. Check his breathing regularly.

Bug alert: **2**

Ticks

A distant cousin to spiders and scorpions, these tiny, eight legged blood suckers are hungry little monsters and they're not fussy what they feed on. Which means that, given the opportunity to bite you, any diseases and infections they've picked up from the birds, mammals and even reptiles, they've already feasted on, can pass into your bloodstream and infect you. Lyme disease is one of these infections.

Ticks are most active from April to October but, during warmer winters and in some parts of the UK, can quest for blood throughout the year. Lack of moisture can be fatal because their bodies dry out easily, so they're not keen on hot, dry summers or very cold or dry winters. They prefer slightly moist, shady areas such as grass, bracken, bushes and leaf litter – the ideal environment for the animals they feed on – and they are least likely to live in short grass or dry heather.

As the adult tick begins to feed, its body fills with blood, and it becomes lighter, almost grey in colour, swelling to the size of a small pea. They can attach anywhere on your body, so check armpits, groin, navel, neck and head. On children, ticks are often found on the head at the hairline. That said, the first sign you've been bitten may be a small bump on the skin which gradually gets bigger.

Early symptoms of Lyme disease include tiredness, chills, fever, headache, muscle and joint pain, swollen lymph glands and blurred vision. If you feel ill, or develop a rash or fever after a tick bite, see a doctor as soon as possible. Go to **www.lymediseaseaction.org.uk** for more information.

53

What you can do... if you're bitten by a tick

● **To remove a tick** gently grasp the tick, as close to the skin as possible with pointed tweezers, without squeezing the tick's body, and pull the tick out without twisting – there may be considerable resistance. Then cleanse the site with antiseptic.

Save the tick in a container, in case you develop symptoms later, labelled with date and location.

TOP tip

No tweezers?

Tie a single loop of cotton around the tick's mouthparts, as close to the skin as possible, then pull gently upwards and outwards.

Bug alert!
Ticks at large!

Taking care in the mountains

DIY tick check

**Ticks prefer warm, moist, dark areas of the body.
A magnifying glass may be helpful.**

- Check clothing for ticks on a frequent basis.
- Check all of your body for ticks. It may be helpful to have someone else inspect your back or other areas which are difficult to see.

  Be sure to include parts that bend such as the backs of knees, between fingers and toes and underarms and pressure points where clothing presses against skin such as underwear elastic, belts, collars and neckties.

- Other common areas include belly button, around or in the ear, hairline or top of the head. If you are by yourself, use a mirror.

Visit the Tick Alert website for further information on tick disease and prevention www.tickalert.org

Photo: Tom Graty

What not to do

● **Avoid squeezing or twisting** the body of the tick – the head may separate from the body, remaining embedded in your skin.

● **Avoid using your fingernails** – infection can enter via even tiny breaks in your skin.

● **Avoid crushing the tick's body** – it may regurgitate its infected stomach contents into the bite wound. Yuk!

● **Don't try to burn off the tick** or apply petroleum jelly, nail polish or any other chemical. Any of these can cause discomfort to the tick, resulting in regurgitation or saliva release.

Precautions you can take

● **Avoid wearing shorts, tuck trousers into socks** in rural and wooded areas and wear strong boots. Ticks grab onto feet and legs and then climb up. Cover exposed skin with protective clothing.

● **Wear light coloured clothing** – ticks are more easily spotted against a light background.

● **Inspect your skin and clothes often** while walking through a tick habitat and at the end of a trip, and remove as soon as possible.

● **Use an insect repellent that is effective against ticks** – applying to shoes, socks, cuffs and trouser legs for maximum effect.

Bug alert!
Ticks at large!

Taking
care in the
mountains

57

PAUL TAYLOR AND TOBY THE SPRINGER
DROPPED OFF ON BLEAKLOW
Photo: Dave Morgan

What you can do if... a helicopter arrives before the rescue team

● **Extinguish all flames and secure all equipment**. The downdraught can knock you over, so make sure you are in a safe position.

● To attract the attention of the helicopter, stand facing it with both arms up in the air making a 'Y' shape.

● Do not approach the helicopter until clearly signalled to do so by the pilot.

What to do
if the
helicopter
arrives

Use the backlight

You're stranded up the mountain in the dark, you can see the helicopter but they can't see you. Try pointing the mobile phone in the direction of the aircraft. Let the backlight guide them to you. Double top tip – it works with your iPod too!

What you can do if... you get lost

Getting lost is usually avoidable. Check your position on the map frequently, especially prior to climbing into mist. Take note of landmarks, time the journey in manageable sections, and check your watch regularly. Use and trust your compass. When it's for real is the wrong time to practise these skills – make them a habit.

If you do get lost, don't panic. Take a few moments to gather your wits then think about how you might 'unlose' yourself.

Establish where you believe you are from your last known position. Take a look around and match what you see with the landmarks on your map to build up a picture of your location. If there's nothing obvious, try walking back the way you came to a recognisable point.

Use the compass to work out which direction to take and, before you set off, check your conclusions a second time.

If you are in mist, try dropping in height until you can see more clearly but beware of suddenly steepening ground. Think back to what the ground was like before you lost your way and judge from this which way to go. Monitor your distance and direction so you can return to your present location.

Match the surrounding terrain to the contour lines on the map, taking note of forestation, rocks and ridge lines, and suchlike. Then try walking towards a 'collecting feature', an obvious feature such as a ridge or river that will 'collect' you as you travel towards it.

What you can do if... it goes dark and you're stuck on the hill

Keep calm. Find shelter. Stay together. Use your spare clothing and survival bag. Eat food and keep morale high. Keep watch for search parties and be ready to attract their attention.

Overflow

Take care using streams to guide you downhill – remember they frequently take shortcuts over precipices!

what happens if...

What to do
if you get
lost or are
benighted

Search and rescue dogs

If you've been reported missing, the chances are there's a search dog and handler in the forward search party.

A SARDA trained dog will tend to ignore moving humans and avoid loose dogs – so stay where you are and tie up your four legged friend! **Why?** The way a search dog operates is through return indication. It's likely to 'find' a long way from its handler and keep returning until its owner makes up the distance between you. Plus, your tied up pooch is more likely to bark and attract the attention of the rescue team.

What you can do if... a member of your party goes missing

Sometimes, with the best of intentions, a member of your party becomes separated from the group. Maybe they stopped – despite our best advice – for some lunch, or a 'scenic break', thinking they'd catch up later. Maybe they took a wrong turning and now can't find their way back to the group. Or perhaps you've done your own thing today, preferring to shop than go on the hill and now you are the one waiting back at the hotel, youth hostel or car park in the gathering gloom, with no signal on the mobile, wondering where your friends are?

If a party is overdue, or someone appears to be missing, it's never an easy decision when to call for help. However, it's probably better to err on the side of caution.

Contact the police through the 999 system as usual, tell them your concerns and let them assess the situation with the team leader of the appropriate rescue team. They will decide whether to initiate a search and when and where to begin searching – usually within a one kilometre radius of the last known point.

But, please do remember that mountain rescue team members are all volunteers and frequently put their own family commitments on hold to search for missing persons. So, if you or your missing party member do manage to make it down alone and unharmed, after a search has been initiated, please do inform the police and rescue team.

Bear in mind that while you're telling your tales of derring-do back in the warmth and safety of the bar, there may be thirty or so mountain rescuers up on the hill in appalling weather, still looking for you!

What to do
if one of
your party
is missing

What you can do if... you have to cross a stream or river

Many people suffer fatal accidents whilst fording streams and rivers, especially those swollen by heavy rain or snow melt. The best way to tackle the problem is very simple – plan your route to avoid having to ford any obstacle. Water levels can rise very quickly and you may be faced with a lengthy detour to avoid crossing a river. Judgements have to be made based on weather conditions, the fitness and experience of the party, time, kit available, an emergency situation etc. Whatever the circumstances, crossing must be seen as a last resort or emergency action – this is not only a high risk activity but very uncomfortable!

Here are some basic pointers:–

● Make a detour upstream to reduced water, if possible.

● Wear boots, but remove socks and trousers.

● Cross diagonally downstream.

● Use a rope to protect the person crossing. But beware, rope can be a safeguard if the right sort of system is used but dangerous if used incorrectly.

● The person crossing should use a stick or branch to feel their way across.

● If you have no rope, stand one behind the other, heaviest at number two, facing upstream. Link hands and shuffle sideways across, taking alternate steps.

● Have your rucksack on by one shoulder strap only, so you can get rid of it if you slip. Make sure the waist strap is also undone.

What you can do if... you're caught or lost in a blizzard

Find or build a temporary shelter or dig a snow hole before any of the party is exhausted or gets cold. Exhaustion and cold together are killers.

Magnet
meets ice axe

If you're trying to navigate out of trouble, keep your ice axe away from the compass. It may affect its accuracy.

What to do if you have to cross water

What you can do if... you meet snow and ice

Snow and ice, plus reduced daylight hours, can change a pleasant four hour stroll in the summer to something of an epic in midwinter. Paths which normally pose no danger can change overnight with many real hazards formed by the ground conditions. A good example is the Llanberis path up Snowdon and the dangerous snow slopes that can build up on it for most of the winter.

Having the correct kit to hand is vital, along with an understanding of its limitations and inherent problems. Most waterproof jackets and trousers are very slippery if you fall on snow or ice. Carrying an ice axe offers some protection (but only if you know what to do with it, so practice on a safe slope) and crampons can be invaluable.

Keep warm stay cool

It's windy and you're getting cold, wishing you'd put that extra thermal on before you set off. How to add an extra mid layer without losing your jacket to the four winds? Easy. Unzip the jacket from the neck down leaving a few inches zipped at the bottom. Take your arms out and tie the sleeves round your waist. Now pop on that extra layer, untie the jacket sleeves, replace arms and zip up. Jacket safe!

65

top tip

Crampon code

Attach crampons – and take out your ice axe – well before you pass the point of safety, when the whole effort becomes a balancing act and you risk losing a vital piece of kit (or your life!) down a very slippery slope.

Carrying survival equipment is very important as the odds of an accident are higher in these conditions. Adding a sleeping bag to everyone's list makes good sense.

That said, good snow conditions can enable you to travel quite quickly, in full control. Glissading can help on downhill sections, but beware unless you know the ground and snow.

● Always think several steps ahead. What lies round the next corner? Will the path become more icy or obscured by snow?

● Be aware that weather conditions can change quickly in the mountains, and darkness falls early in the winter – even earlier if the day was murky from the start. With darkness come falling temperatures. And it can become dramatically colder as you climb higher.

● If you must remove a glove, make sure it's secure by clipping it onto a zipper, or stuff it down the front of your jacket.

What to do
if you meet
ice and
snow

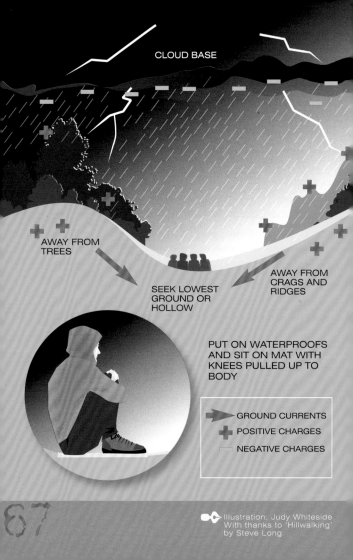

CLOUD BASE

AWAY FROM TREES

SEEK LOWEST GROUND OR HOLLOW

AWAY FROM CRAGS AND RIDGES

PUT ON WATERPROOFS AND SIT ON MAT WITH KNEES PULLED UP TO BODY

➡ GROUND CURRENTS

✚ POSITIVE CHARGES

▬ NEGATIVE CHARGES

67

Illustration: Judy Whiteside
With thanks to 'Hillwalking'
by Steve Long

What you can do if... a storm threatens

High on a mountain is a dangerous place to be during a storm – as the recent tragic death of a hillwalker struck by lightning near a summit in the Southern Highlands has shown – even though the chances of being struck by lightning are small. Mountain Leader Training UK publish the following advice in their book 'Hillwalking', by Steve Long, reproduced here with their permission.

Lightning strikes rarely come as a bolt out of the blue. Towering clouds build up as unstable air spirals upwards and condenses, giving a good warning to the observant walker. As a storm approaches, its location can be estimated by noting the difference in time between lightning flashes and the rumble of thunder. The light appears almost simultaneously, while sound travels at a speed of 1 km per 3 seconds. A six second delay therefore means that the storm is about two kilometres away.

Lightning strikes are quite frequent on summits and other projections such as pinnacles, because lightning takes the shortest route to earth. These are the areas of greatest risk and, at the first sign of an approaching lightning storm, the party should evacuate to a safer area. Scrambling terrain is particularly hazardous in lightning, and difficult to escape from quickly. A

What to do if a storm threatens

Thunder and lightning

Head for shelter as soon as you see distant lightning or hear thunder. Lightning often precedes rain – so don't wait for the rain to come before taking action.

Avoid water, high ground and open spaces.

Avoid metal objects such as electric wires and machinery and bear in mind that walking poles strapped to rucksacks can act as handy lightning conductors!

Avoid sheltering under trees, crags and ridges.

If one of your party is struck by lightning make everyone safe, administer first aid and call for help as soon as possible. Injured people do not carry an electric charge.

strike could easily knock somebody from his or her footing. Retreat should definitely not be by abseil, because the wet rope provides an excellent conductor. Steep or exposed ground should therefore be avoided if storms are forecast, or at least be pre-empted by a very early start and finish.

Direct lightning strikes on people are relatively rare, but can be extremely violent and often fatal. More common is a partial strike, either through induction from an adjacent or nearby conductor, or through the ground as the earth currents dissipate outwards. The actual power of the stroke is a combination of the current and the contact time.

A projection such as a pinnacle or post acts as a lightning conductor that services an area with a radius corresponding approximately to its own height. This means that the area within this circumference is a relatively safe place to wait because the projection will deflect lightning strikes on itself.

Sheltering under an overhang or a tree is a hazardous course of action because a lightning strike will bridge the gap taking the most economical route, in this case through the people and into the ground. It is much safer to sit out in the open wearing waterproofs.

A walking party sitting out a lightning storm should ideally crouch or sit upright on top of insulating material such as rucksacks and sleeping mats. Hands should be kept on knees rather than touching the ground. Metal items of equipment do not significantly increase the risk of attracting a strike, but if they start to hum and spark, it would be wise to accept the hint and lay them to one side until the storm passes.

© **Steve Long**
From 'Hillwalking' by Steve Long. Published by Mountain Leader Training UK. Reproduced here with thanks.

What to do
if a storm
threatens

What you can do if... you're caught in an avalanche

Many avalanche accidents are caused by climbers attempting routes during, or shortly after, a heavy snowfall which has fallen on older snow or after a sudden thaw. Various types of slab avalanche and wet snow avalanche are the most common and their danger and frequency should never be underestimated. New or drifting snow accumulates as soft or hard slab under the influence of the wind, particularly in the lee of ridges and other natural features.

The golden rule is not to climb within 24 hours of a heavy snowfall. However, you should remember that good knowledge of the previous week's weather is also important. High winds some time before could have produced windslab slopes which could still be dangerous, particularly if a stable cold period has existed since, so a good understanding of windslab and its significance is also advisable.

This is one of the few incidents when you should NOT go for the rescue team. The effort you and your companions put into the immediate search could be the avalanche victim's best chance of survival. Life expectancy after half an hour drops to 50% so the first hour is crucial. If avalanche cords or transceivers are being used your task should be relatively straightforward.

71

Immediate action

● Check for further danger. Your first concern should be for the safety of you and your party.

● Mark the last seen point of the victim.

● Quick search – listening carefully and looking for any signs (mittens, hats, rucksack).

● Mark the point carefully and do not remove any items found – these may be useful clues to the fall line of a submerged avalanche victim.

● Undertake a thorough search.

One hour later

● Send for further help. If you had a reasonably large party, you might have sent for help earlier, but never at the expense of an immediate search being undertaken.

● Remove any casualties to a place which is safe from further avalanche. Check and clear their nose and mouth. All avalanche victims should be insulated from the cold ground (or snow) and should be treated for hypothermia and shock. Partially submerged victims should be pulled from the snow very quickly.

What to do
if you're
avalanched

Avalanche

If you're caught in an avalanche you may not have the time, opportunity or presence of mind to take defensive action. That said, the following could buy you precious minutes as the rescue team search the surface.

- Plunging an ice axe into the undersurface may help to keep you near the top of the slide.
- Swim. If you can't escape the fall, swimming may improve your chances of emerging nearer the surface. Your body is far denser than avalanche debris so you are likely to sink unless you swim hard.
- As the avalanche slows, push a hand upwards. Visual clues will help your friends – and rescuers – find you faster.
- Spit. You may not know which way is up. Try spitting then watching where it falls. It may just give you a clue.
- Keep one hand in front of your face to clear an airspace. This will delay the build up of carbon dioxide in the snow around your mouth, helping you breath for longer.
- Try to maintain sufficient space for chest expansion by taking and holding a deep breath.

Once the avalanche comes to a halt, it will immediately set like concrete around you, so any defensive actions must be taken BEFORE it stops. Unless you are very near the surface or have a hand sticking up out of the snow, it will be almost impossible to dig yourself out.

Checking out the mountain weather

Weather is probably one of the most important issues for those venturing into the mountain environment. A high proportion of serious incidents involving climbers and walkers occur because those involved have not prepared adequately for the conditions they might face or were simply caught out by the capricious nature of mountain weather. What started out as a beautiful sunny day, inspiring tee shirts and shorts, can quickly turn to lowering fog or blizzard conditions, with zero visibility and rapidly falling temperatures.

You should make every effort to gather as much information on actual and forecast conditions before you set off. But beware. Many routine weather observations are made from populated, low lying areas of the British Isles and actual weather reports from mountainous areas are often scarce. Look for local sources and learn to read the signs of changing conditions.

The Met Office

www.metoffice.gov.uk provides mountain weather forecasts for the following areas:–

- Scottish West Highlands
- Scottish East Highlands
- Lake District National Park
- Yorkshire Dales National Park
- Peak District National Park
- Snowdonia National Park
- Brecon Beacons National Park

Forecasts are issued twice daily, cover daylight hours and contain the following information:–

- Hazard risk
- Three-hourly weather summary
- Probability of precipitation
- Hill fog and visibility
- Maximum wind speeds
- Temperatures in the valley and at the summit
- Latest pressure chart
- A general outlook for the next few days

A variety of downloadable weather gadgets are available, to keep you up to date with changing weather patterns, and you can receive weather forecasts on the move with the 'Met Office Weather' app for the iPhone.

But remember that rapidly changing conditions can quickly render mountain weather reports out of date, so always check for the latest available forecast. National and local media may not be detailed enough for specific mountain areas but local information boards can be invaluable.

The Mountain Weather Information Service

www.mwis.org.uk provides detailed weather forecasts for eight areas of the UK:–

- North West Highlands of Scotland
- West Highlands of Scotland
- Cairngorms National Park and Monadhliath
- South East Highlands of Scotland
- Southern Uplands of Scotland
- Lake District
- Peak District and Yorkshire Dales
- Snowdonia National Park

Forecasts are freely available for downloading as Adobe PDF files, or via internet enabled mobile phones. Users are encouraged to print and freely distribute or publicly display them for the benefit of all hill-goers.

All forecasts are produced seven days a week, 52 weeks a year. Each forecast is released between 2pm and 4pm and covers the following three days.

77

sportscotland Avalanche Information Service

www.sais.gov.uk provides daily forecasts of the snow, avalanche and climbing conditions, during the winter season, for five areas of Scotland:–

- Creag Meagaidh
- Glencoe
- Lochaber
- Northern Cairngorms
- Southern Cairngorms

Forecasts detail hazard scale from 1 (Very Low) to 5 (Very High), with information on snow pack stability and the possibility of avalanche, and advice for off piste and back country activities.

The SAIS also welcome your feedback on snow conditions and avalanche activity, if possible on the day of observation. You can use the avalanche recording form on the website or phone transferred charge to the SAIS office on 01479 861264.

Wind

Dominated by topography, this normally increases with height and can be funnelled and accelerated through valleys and gaps or forced across hilltops, producing gusty and turbulent conditions. Wind chill is an important consideration, especially in the colder and windier winter months. Settled conditions will often allow light downslope (katabatic) winds to form at night, and upslope (anabatic) winds early in the day.

Temperature

Normally decreases with height, on average three degrees per 1000ft, but higher levels are sometimes warmer when cold air is trapped in lower lying areas. Freezing levels are rarely uniform in mountainous areas, and will often slowly lower in persistent precipitation. Temperatures on south facing slopes will often rise more rapidly than valley floors in spring and summer, allowing fog and low cloud to rise up the hillside.

Cloud

Usually, but not always, this is lowest on windward facing slopes, with an often much higher base to the lee of highest ground. Hill fog is an obvious hazard, but cloud bases are seldom uniform over mountainous areas. Local winds and differential surface heating will often produce significant variations in base height and amounts.

Rain and snow

Freezing level is obviously crucial for change of type between rain and snow. Remember the snow level often steadily lowers in more persistent and heavy rain, due to evaporative cooling. Warm spells in summer can often trigger heavy showers or thunderstorms, with localised flash flooding. Look out for significant vertical build up of cloud during the day.

There will we sit upon the rocks
And see the shepherds feed their flocks
By shallow rivers, to whose falls
Melodious birds sing madrigals

Christopher Marlowe ✒

81

Where you can go, what you can do

Public rights of way

The public 'rights of way' criss crossing our towns and countryside are legal highways providing tens of thousands of miles of footpaths, tracks, bridleways and byways for you to enjoy at any time. Some also have extra rights to ride a horse, cycle or drive a vehicle. You will find them marked on OS maps, detailed in guidebooks or waymarked by arrows en route.

A **yellow arrow** indicates a path for use by walkers only. You may also use a wheelchair or invalid carriage, a pram or a pushchair here but it is illegal to cycle, ride a horse or drive a vehicle without the landowner's permission. You may usually take a dog, provided it is kept under control.

A **blue arrow** indicates a bridleway, open to walkers, horse riders and cyclists.

A **dark red arrow** indicates a restricted byway, open to walkers, cyclists, horses and horse-drawn vehicles.

A **red arrow** indicates a byway open to all traffic (BOAT).

Follow The
Countryside Code

The code consists of five sections dedicated to helping you respect, protect and enjoy the countryside.

- Be safe, plan ahead and follow any signs
- Leave gates and property as you find them – use gates and stiles where provided rather than climbing over walls and hedges
- Protect plants and animals and take your litter home – even those banana skins
- Keep dogs under close control
- Consider other people

National Trails

There are currently fifteen National Trails in England and Wales and four in Scotland, where they are called Long Distance Routes. All the trails are suitable for walkers, with some sections suited to cyclists, horse riders and people of limited mobility. For more information, visit **www.nationaltrail.co.uk**.

Open access land

Since the CROW Act came into effect, walkers and outdoor enthusiasts have also been able to explore huge areas of previously inaccessible countryside, across England and Wales, without having to stick to paths.

Always check for restrictions before setting out, and respect local signage or requests by estate staff. For a complete guide to the code, and to view the Open Access Maps, go to **www.naturalengland.org.uk** and follow the links for countryside visitors. Once you're out there, look for the Open Access symbol, guiding you to entry and exit points.

Most of the recreational activities you can do on foot, you can do on access land. So walking, sightseeing, birdwatching, climbing and running are allowed – with a few common sense restrictions in place which limit where you can walk or take a dog.

Cycling, camping, horse riding or driving (except buggies or mobility scooters) are not allowed unless these activities already take place, or the landowner has given consent.

Landowners may also restrict or exclude the public from their land for up to 28 days each year if necessary, for any reason.

Your dog and the great outdoors

What better way to enjoy the open air than alongside your four legged friend? In general, there's no need to keep your dog on a lead on public paths as long as it is within your sight and under close control.

But if you're planning to explore the areas of moorland and mountain newly registered as access land, check the map to ensure dogs are allowed. Land marked in yellow is fine, red hatching means you should check details of the restriction to see whether it affects you.

You should use a fixed lead at all times near livestock – no more than 2 metres (6 foot) long – and during the ground nesting bird season, between 1 March and 31 July. Dogs may also be excluded from grouse moors and from lambing enclosures during the lambing season.

Many rare birds build their nests on the moors. Disturbed by people and dogs, trampling through their habitat, they may abandon their nests, leaving their eggs and chicks to the mercy of the elements and predators, or simply become exhausted and die.

Your dog and other animals

It may be your dog's natural instinct to chase things, but this can cause distress and even fatal injury for the animals concerned. Animals will instinctively protect themselves and their young so it pays to look ahead and keep your dog on a lead if you are likely to encounter livestock.

Cows, we need hardly say, are big creatures and there have been reported incidents involving walkers and cattle. If you're concerned about crossing a field of cows, check the map to find another way round. If there's no alternative or, if you're mid-field and feeling threatened by cows, walk – don't run – to the nearest field exit, keeping as far from them as possible.

If a farm animal chases you, let your dog off the lead to get away and distract the animal away from you – don't put yourself at risk trying to protect your dog. Whether injured or not, you should report the incident to the Health and Safety Executive on 0845 300 9923.

And, finally, contact with dog faeces can cause serious bacterial infections in people and animals, and damage the delicate chemical balance of our environment. Please, clear up your dog's mess and dispose of it responsibly – either take it home or place in the bins provided.

BLUEBELLS AT RANNERDALE, CUMBRIA
Photo: Judy Whiteside

Smoking and fire risk

● **Check for fire restrictions before setting out, respect warning signs and never extinguish a cigarette on open ground.**

Moorland fire presents a huge threat to the fragility of the moors. Seventy five per cent of heather moorland is in the British Isles – rarer than the tropical rain forest – and recent years have seen fires devastate large tracts of ground, sometimes burning right down into the peat and destroying the seed bank.

These areas will take hundreds of years to recover, but there is a wider ecological implication. Moorland peat holds in huge amounts of carbon and, once disturbed, this is exposed to the atmosphere. The bare peat on our moors contributes substantially to pollution. To protect our heather moorland and its fragile eco system visitors are asked not to smoke on or near the moors when at fire risk.

*Areas shown are approximate

Mountain and cave rescue teams and regions

Lake District Search & Rescue (LDSAMRA)

Cockermouth MRT
Coniston MRT
COMRU (Mines Rescue)
Duddon & Furness MRT
Kendal MRT
Keswick MRT
Kirkby Stephen MRT
Langdale/Ambleside MRT
Patterdale MRT
Penrith MRT
Wasdale MRT
SARDA (Lakes)

Mid Pennine Search & Rescue Organisation (MPSRO)

Bolton MRT
Bowland Pennine MRT
Calder Valley SRT
Cave Rescue Organisation
Holme Valley MRT
Rossendale & Pendle MRT
SARDA (England)

North East Search & Rescue Association (NESRA)

Cleveland SRT
North of Tyne SRT
Northumberland NPSRT
RAF Leeming MRT
Scarborough & District SRT
Swaledale FRO
Teesdale & Weardale SRT
SARDA (England)

North Wales Mountain Rescue Association (NWMRA)

Aberglaslyn MRT
Llanberis MRT
North East Wales SRT
North Wales CRO
Ogwen Valley MRO
Outward Bound Wales SRT
SARDA (Wales)
Snowdonia National Park
South Snowdonia SRT
HM Coastguard MRT 83
RAF Valley MRT

Mountain and cave rescue teams and regions

Peak District Mountain Rescue Organisation (PDMRO)

Buxton MRT
Derbyshire CRO
Derby MRT
Edale MRT
Glossop MRT
Kinder MRT
Oldham MRT
Woodhead MRT
SARDA (England)

Peninsula Mountain & Cave Rescue Association (PenMaCRA)

Cornwall SRT
Dartmoor SRT (Ashburton)
Dartmoor SRT (Okehampton)
Dartmoor SRT (Plymouth)
Dartmoor SRT (Tavistock)
Devon CRO
Exmoor SRT
SARDA (England)

South Wales Search & Rescue Association (SWSRA)

Brecon MRT
Central Beacons MRT
Gwent CRT
Longtown MRT
West Brecon CRT
Western Beacons MSRT
SARDA (South Wales)

South West England Rescue Association (SWERA)

Avon & Somerset SAR
Gloucester CRG
Mendip Cave Rescue
Severn Area RA

Yorkshire Dales Rescue Panel (YDRP)

Upper Wharfedale FRA
RAF Leeming MRT
Cave Rescue Organisation

How the call out system works

So... you've dialled 999 and asked for mountain rescue. What happens next?

Mountain rescue teams are called out through the police, via the 999 system, so your call will be routed to the police control room in the area of the incident. Depending on the information given, it may also be routed to another emergency service such as the ambulance service or air ambulance. It is key to the rapid evacuation and recovery of any casualties that you provide as much information as possible about the accident, and the location and nature of the terrain.

The team nearest to the incident will then be contacted and team members alerted via page or mobile phone by their team leader. A 'spot pick up', such as an injured walker on the hill, may be undertaken by a small 'hasty' group of just sufficient members to locate and treat the casualty before rapid transfer to a helicopter. Others may require more team members to carry the stretcher over difficult terrain for a longer period of time, before a helicopter or land ambulance can take over. Sometimes, team members will transfer the casualty direct to hospital in their team vehicle.

A search for a missing person requires more planning and personnel. The police search managers will work with the team leader and informants to gather as much detail as possible to create an informed search strategy.

93

KESWICK TEAM MEMBERS AND
CASUALTY AWAIT THE HELICOPTER
Photo: Keswick MRT

Frequently, the team leader will merely advise possible search strategy before team members are called – which may be sufficient to resolve the situation. In other cases, team leaders may be able to guide a 'lost' person down from the hill, over the phone, without a full team call out.

Mountain rescue teams often work with search dogs and handlers from the Search and Rescue Dog Association. Handlers are fully trained mountain rescue team members who undertake further training with their dogs. They are especially useful in bad weather and at night, when the chances of a team member finding a casualty, other than close to a path, may be severely reduced unless the missing person can attract attention.

Once a casualty is located, the first team members on scene will assess the situation and safety of everyone involved, take a history and carry out a head to toe examination, noting injuries and vital signs before giving appropriate first aid treatment and pain relief. Meanwhile, other team members will assemble the necessary equipment to stretcher the casualty in warmth and comfort to the ambulance, and liaise with the emergency services or RAF SAR to evacuate them from the hill as quickly as possible. If a prolonged stretcher carry is required, team members will work in relays to literally spread the load, meanwhile continuing to monitor the casualty's condition and wellbeing.

Bring me men
to match my
mountains.
Bring me men
to match my
plains. Men with
empires in their
purpose and
new eras
in their brains.
Sam Walter
Foss

95

From the mountains to mountain rescue

Mountain rescue wasn't always the professional, world class service it is today. Indeed, there was barely a perceived need for it in any form, organised or otherwise.

Hill walking and climbing for pleasure were the prerogative of the rich – the gentlemen and ladies who could afford to be adventurous with their time, money and life. Those less fortunate may have worked in the mountains, working the farmsteads, herding cattle, building roads and walls, quarrying tin or slate or hunting wild game for food. But these things were born of necessity, not pleasure, and a need to earn a living.

Those who were injured in the mountains either died at the scene of their misfortune, from their injuries or exposure hypothermia, or relied on their companions to rally local farmers, shepherds and quarrymen into makeshift rescue parties using makeshift equipment, and possibly died anyway, their injuries made worse by the journey across rough terrain, without the benefit of pain relief or protection from the elements.

Birth of the mountaineering club

Things began to change in the late eighteenth century, aided and abetted by writers such as Wordsworth and Ruskin, and artists like William Bellers and Thomas Smith, painting pictures with words and watercolour to inspire the aspirant traveller. Cumbrian born William Gilpin recorded his appreciation of the wild and rugged mountains in his travel journals. At a time when improving road communications here, and travel restrictions across Europe, had prompted an explosion in domestic tourism, his books were ideal for the new generation of traveller. In Wales, Cambridge student William Bingley explored the cliffs and ledges of Snowdonia in search of botanical specimens. And in Scotland, any forays into the mountains were reserved for the very fit with a good deal of time on their hands.

The inspiration to climb in Europe was initially rooted more in the search for geological evidence and the study of glacial movement than the desire to climb. In the early nineteenth century, James Forbes, a professor of natural philosophy at Edinburgh university – and widely recognised as the inaugurator of Scottish mountaineering – was instrumental in stimulating British interest in the Alps. His detailed descriptions and sketches, as his research into the flow of glaciers took him to the mountains of France, Switzerland and Norway, captured the public imagination and whet the appetite for travel.

As the sport grew, so too did the desire to share experiences with others. The Alpine Club, formed in 1857, became the forerunner for the mountaineering clubs which would spring up across the UK over the next fifty years or so – the very backbone of the mountain rescue service.

By the time Edward Whymper made the first ascent of the seemingly impregnable Matterhorn in July 1865, the simple enjoyment of the hills and mountains, both at home and abroad, was firmly established as a national pastime.

Whymper's own engravings in 'Scrambles Among the Alps', depict men dressed in thin woollen jackets and trousers, jaunty hats and leather boots and carrying tiny rucksacks, the women climbing with them swathed in long petticoats and frilled blouses. It was the standard wear of the mountaineer at home and abroad. How anyone climbed to altitude at all – let alone survived – seems nothing short of miraculous when you consider the technical clothing and equipment deemed necessary today. And there would be little change as the twentieth century dawned and matured. The novice climber invariably set out on his adventures in a pair of hob-nailed boots, fashioned to the best of his ability with hammer and nails – though even these might be removed in favour of stockinged feet on the more difficult rocks – later progressing to alpine nails such as the ring clinker and the tricouni. On steep dry rock, the plimsoll was king.

There was some equipment available but technology had not yet conceived the karabiners or chalk pouches of today's climber. Hemp rope was the norm, which tended to be stiff and unforgiving when wet, and the standard belay technique consisted of wrapping the rope round the waist or diagonally up the back and over the shoulder. The average mountaineer relied on a combination of tweed cloth and heavy knits for protection from the elements, a jacket of oiled cloth if he was lucky.

And they were a hard bunch those climbers, the tradition that 'the leader did not fall'. If by chance they lost their balance, they knew the risks. Perhaps it never occurred to these adventurers that they might die, driven as they were to climb, to discover, to meet the challenge. But when they fell, they expected to be rescued by their fellow climbers.

The birth of the mountaineering club

History

ABSEILING WITHOUT
THE AID OF KARABINER

This spirit of self-reliance – at the heart of mountain rescue – continued to grow as climbers found different ways to climb. The point was not merely to reach the summit but to meet the challenges of getting there. Still though, mountaineering retained something of an elitist air. Few considered it a sport to be undertaken for no other reason than the sheer pleasure of physical exercise. But, as the domestic climbing scene opened up, an activity which had once been the dominion of the leisured upper classes began to attract more men and women from the growing middle classes. With this came the acceptance of climbing as an end in itself.

In 1889, the Scottish Mountaineering Club – the very first domestic club – had begun to energise the Scottish climbing community, mainly through winter climbing. The Climbers Club, established in 1898 to facilitate the development of Welsh rock climbing, produced the first pocket climbing guide in 1909.

In the years leading up to and following the First World War, men such as George Mallory and Geoffrey Winthrop Young spent their weekends in search of new routes in the Lakes and Wales. And, when time could not be spared to travel, the gritstone of Derbyshire beckoned.

Then, in 1903, a tragic accident high on Scafell Pinnacle – the worst British climbing history had known – saw four climbers, tied together as they climbed, fall together to their death as their leader slipped. The 'Scafell Disaster' was perhaps a pivotal moment in mountain rescue history as a shocked climbing fraternity began to consider the increasing incidence of mountain accidents and the lack of rescue resources available. Within a year, first aid and mountain rescue equipment – albeit rudimentary by today's standards – began to appear in key areas, such as the Gorphwysfa Hotel at Pen y Pass, in Snowdonia.

Many of the climbing pioneers were city dwellers, escaping from their work as doctors and dons at the great hospitals and universities. And it was in Manchester, several hours journey by road or rail from the mountains, where the Rucksack Club was formed in 1902. Four years later, Lake District mountaineers joined forces as the Fell and Rock Climbing Club.

The birth of the mountaineering club

History

103

An accident occurs

The seeds of mountain rescue were germinating but it was an accident in 1928, at Laddow Rocks in the Peak District, and the extreme difficulties encountered by rescuers, which sparked their rapid growth and the eventual formation of the Mountain Rescue Committee.

Edgar Pryor, an ex-president of the Rucksack Club, was a forceful character reported to have

the back story

occurs

History

104

'come to the mountains like a meteor, who would not follow if he could not lead'. The accident occurred on the Rucksack Club meet after the annual dinner in November, when Pryor was knocked off the upper stance on the Long Climb at Laddow by a lady climber, who was not in the party, falling down the upper pitch. It was a rough hillside, covered with steep rocks, and Pryor fell about 40 feet into an adjacent gully breaking his skull and thigh bone. Herbert Hartley, who had just become a member of the Rucksack Club by special dispensation for his youthful age of eighteen, and who later became secretary and statistician for the MRC, took part in a relay of runners bringing up blankets and hot water bottles from Crowden. Dr Findlay, a police surgeon and club member who was attending the meet, devised a splint from a rucksack frame and organised evacuation of the casualty from Crowden, using the finger post from the Crowden path as a stretcher.

Despite the ingenuity and care in the improvisation of stretcher and splint, it was an agonising business. The nearest place on the road to which the ambulance could be taken involved carrying the patient for four hours, using relays of stretcher bearers. It was rough going almost all the way and, on reaching the ambulance, Pryor faced a further one and a half hour journey to the Manchester Royal Infirmary.

Fortunately the weather was good but, had it been rough and stormy, he would have arrived in worse condition. Delivered to the Infirmary, he came under the care of Wilson Hey, consulting surgeon, who later observed that the casualty was so shocked he needed blood transfusion before he could be operated on, and that the transport and shock had so damaged the limb, he was forced to amputate some months later. 'The absence of morphia with the transport had done more damage to the limb than the mountain', he said. As a result of his experience, Hey began to agitate for the formation of an organised mountain rescue service with the assistance of morphia, which he regarded as essential.

In fact, improvised splints and stretchers were the norm. Hey, a keen and experienced climber himself, had witnessed the inventiveness of mountain rescue at first hand when climbing with two medical friends on the Glyders in North Wales. Near the summit of Glyder Fach they came across a man with a broken leg in need of urgent medical attention. As one kept vigil with the casualty, the other two went to fetch help and a stretcher from the rescue post at Pen y Gwryd. On the way down, they came across a gate which they 'borrowed'. Mindful that time was of the essence, they carried the gate up to the ridge and made the man as comfortable as was

An accident
occurs

History

possible, before fixing him to the 'stretcher' and setting off down the mountain. The journey, needless to say, was traumatic for the casualty – the gate was uncomfortable, their makeshift splint was causing extreme pain to his injured leg, and there were no pain killing drugs available. Further inspiration, were it required, for Hey's determination to improve the treatment of casualties.

An accident in 1931, on Crib Goch in North Wales, brought Alfred Sefton Pigott – one of Britain's most outstanding climbers between the wars – to the same conclusion. As a member of a carrying party which brought the injured man down, he experienced first hand the woefully inadequate equipment – an old stretcher and a few bandages – and the extreme difficulty in bringing the man off the mountain without doing him further harm.

Shortly after the accident, he began to discuss the possibility of forming some kind of rescue organisation with Hey, a fellow member of the Rucksack Club.

TRICOUNI NAILS

Searching for a mountain stretcher

The Rucksack Club created a subcommittee to look into the growing concerns. At the same time, the Fell and Rock Climbing Club formed their own 'stretcher subcommittee' tasked with finding a satisfactory stretcher for mountain rescue purposes. After the first World War, a few ex-army stretchers had been placed in some high risk areas in the hills, but still it was virtually impossible to carry a casualty over rocky ground and down steep scree slopes without danger to both casualty and bearers, or the greatest suffering.

In 1932, the two committees combined to form the Joint Stretcher Committee, charged to produce a suitable mountain stretcher and a list of first aid equipment. Before their report in 1935, the committee of Dr Charles Paget Lapage (chairman), Fred Pigott (secretary), H L Pollitt, Morley Wood, Eustace Thomas and Wilson Hey considered a number of stretchers but it was the Thomas stretcher, designed by Eustace Thomas, which was chosen as most suitable.

A vigorous and enthusiastic walker, Thomas had moved from his native London in 1900, to join his brother's company Bertram Thomas (Engineers) Ltd – perhaps fortunately for mountain rescue, as it was here the stretchers would be manufactured. The original design consisted of wooden runners made of ash, an aluminium frame and a stout canvas bed. Its telescopic handles locked automatically into their extended position, allowing the end carriers to see their feet and avoid stumbling. The

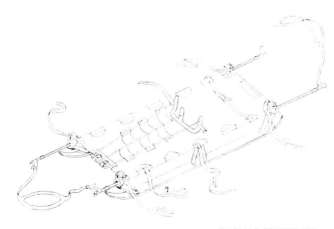

THOMAS STRETCHER

wooden runners gave sufficient ground clearance to allow easy movement across rock, scree, grass or snow, although it was not strong enough to be dragged over very rough ground.

A double Thomas splint, wooden arm splints, iodine, bandages, kettle, primus stove, eiderdown, feeding cup and urine bottle were recommended as vital first aid equipment. The Thomas splint, although sharing the same name, was devised by Hugh Owen Thomas, a noted pioneer in British orthopaedic surgery, whose belief that rest and immobilisation were of more benefit to the patient than excision or amputation, had led him to invent a variety of splints and a wrench for the reduction of fractures.

The prescribed equipment was to be left at designated posts for use by climbers and post supervisors along with local volunteers. Posts were established in some of the more popular climbing areas – such as Glen Brittle on Skye and on Ben Nevis, at Sty Head Tarn in the Lake District and Pen y Gwryd in the Ogwen Valley – and were managed by the mountaineering clubs with the help of donated funds. Each post fell under the supervision of a designated individual. These 'Good Samaritans of the mountain valleys' were said to be the 'foundation of the whole service'. Several post supervisors became outstanding leaders of the ad hoc

Searching
for a mountain
stretcher

History

rescue parties formed as needed. Sid Cross, of the Old Dungeon Ghyll Hotel in Langdale, made many such rescues, averaging one or two a week during the summer, sometimes solo. Similarly, Chris Briggs at Pen y Gwryd in Wales, and Ron James and Tony Mason at Ogwen Cottage. In Scotland, Walter Elliot and his sons were notable for their rescue work in Glencoe.

In September 1936, the committee decided a more permanent structure was called for, to maintain and manage the posts and administer donations. The First Aid Committee of Mountaineering Clubs was born, composed of representatives of the mountaineering clubs, including those of the universities, and bodies with allied interests such as the Ramblers Federation and the Youth Hostel Association. The committee members, all very experienced climbers, and led by Lapage and Piggott, were Wilson Hey (Alpine Club), G G McPhee (Scottish Mountaineering Cub), H W Humphries (Yorkshire Ramblers), W G Pape (Wayfarers), C H French (Climbers Club) and G E Gallimore (Gritstone Club). A central fund was organised from a 2% levy from the clubs and all accidents and use of equipment had to be reported to the committee.

This situation would continue until the summer of 1949 when the Minister of Health and the Secretary of State for Scotland agreed to provide all transport and medical equipment (except morphia) under the National Health Service, through the Manchester Royal Infirmary.

Robert Burns, though not actually a member of the committee, designed and made the stretcher beds and eiderdown covers, produced the rucksacks used to hold the medical supplies and made the necessary repairs and replacements to keep the kit in good order.

In pursuit of morphia

The new committee represented the coming together of respected figures from the worlds of mountaineering and medicine, driven by a single purpose – the survival and comfort of the casualty. It's a purpose which has continued to drive mountain rescue for seventy five years, through a process of experience and innovation. But it was Hey's determined belief in the use of morphia – and its eventual addition to the equipment list – which many consider the most powerful legacy to mountain rescue.

Despite being refused permission by the Home Office in 1934, and convinced in his belief

In pursuit of morphia

History

that 'morphia reduces suffering, and suffering produces shock, and prolonged shock causes death', Hey decided to issue morphia to the posts without a licence, at his own expense. He continued to do so for fifteen years – and made no secret of the fact. Its use was so widely advertised in pamphlets and journals that he freely admitted he almost took for granted that the government would be so impressed with the saving of lives and prevention of suffering, due to the use of morphia, they might overlook the fact that formal permission had not been given.

In the beginning, the drug was administered via ordinary syringes and needles but, in 1938, La Roche Chemical Works provided tubonic ampoule syringes. Instructions for their use were provided in every rucksack and practical training given. Hey's belief was that these same syringes had been used in the field of battle, often by non-medically trained personnel, so why should they not now be administered by non-medically trained civilians in the similarly extenuating circumstances of mountain rescue.

In August 1949, having learned that the drug was now allowed in mines and at airports for use by lay people, Hey reapplied to the Home Office to have issues of morphia legalised.

Five days later, a Mr Dyke from the Home Office arrived to see Hey, without an appointment. Hey agreed to see the visitor

In pursuit of morphia

History

immediately but was astonished to find him accompanied by a detective sergeant. Angry at the impolite manner of his interview, Hey refused to produce the requested Dangerous Drugs Book relating to his dealings with morphia.

Whilst his frequent letters to Whitehall met with a wall of silence, Hey found himself under extreme pressure from the national press, fed by Home Office leaks, to make a statement. In fact, the leaks were so endemic the press were able to inform Hey of his imminent summons for 'wilful obstruction', ten days before it was served. Despite the evident loyalty of some of the better papers, Hey was afraid 'the rag press' would 'make a song' of the whole thing. 'Already they have damaged my reputation considerably. I am thought to be either a drug addict or that I am making money out of selling drugs to addicts.'

He called a Grand Council, including Monkhouse, the assistant editor of the Manchester Guardian, and reluctantly sent a letter to the Home Office. If they were prepared to withdraw the summons, he would withdraw all morphia from mountain rescue posts in Scotland, England and Wales and would not issue any more in the future. As a consulting surgeon, he said, he neither required nor possessed a Dangerous Drugs Book but kept careful records. And anyway, the quantity of morphia missing during the fifteen years 'would not satisfy a morphia addict for a single day!'

Hey was prepared to become a martyr, declaring himself on the warpath. It grieved him that 'Britain is probably the only country in the civilised world where morphia is not provided in organised mountain rescue for those injured when walking and climbing.'

Court proceedings were twice postponed, the charge reduced to obstruction and refusal to produce a drugs book – the maximum penalty a £250 fine and 12 month's imprisonment. The whole affair ended in something of an anti-climax with Hey convicted of the lesser charge and fined a mere £10 with 10 guineas costs, settled by the Mountain Rescue Committee 'for the sake of propaganda'.

Within days, having publicly humiliated a man of exemplary character who had only ever acted with integrity and concern for the casualty, the government performed an about turn. Hey was invited to submit 'another' plan for consideration. As this was the first time he'd actually been asked for any plan at all, he related the procedure to date – mountain morphia stocks were kept in a locked steel safe and rescue kit was in the charge of a supervisor, generally at a hotel, police station or farm. The only exception was a mountain hut on Ben Nevis where it could not be kept under lock and key as it must be ready for use in an emergency. Tubonic

In pursuit of morphia

History

ampoules made overdose impossible and replacement of stocks was not made unless a full report of the accident, with the name and address of the casualty on whom the morphia was used, had been supplied. All equipment was also subject to periodic inspections.

During fifteen years, he noted, he had only lost 1.25grs 'which must be far better than the average of any hospital ward or general practitioner.'

A date was set for a meeting in London, in December, on the eve of the Alpine Club dinner. Wilson Hey and Fred Piggott represented the MRC, along with members of the British Mountaineering Council, the Alpine Club and the

KESWICK MRT c1947
Photo: Dick Fisher

Scottish Mountaineering Club. They were joined by Lord Chorley (thanks to whose efforts Hey reckoned mountain rescue would 'soon be a brilliant performance instead of a shoddy affair'), Sir Cecil Wakeley (President of the Royal College of Surgeons) and Dr Raymond Greene of Bartholomew's Hospital and veteran of Kamet 1931 and Everest 1933.

With the weight of public opinion against them, the Home Office relented on 14 December and agreed to the supply of morphia to mountain rescue posts, provided an annual return was submitted, giving details of issue and use. The supply would be three quarter grain ampoules for each post, except for Ogwen and Glencoe which would have six ampoules each because of the frequency of accidents in those areas. Since that day, mountain rescue has appointed a Medical Officer responsible for the issue of morphia – the first, of course, the redoubtable Wilson Hey.

As the morphia furore reached its denouement, there were developments aplenty to exercise the hearts and minds of mountain rescue. The Ministry of Fuel and Power offered petrol coupons for mountain rescue use, the Ordnance Survey Department agreed to mark the growing number of rescue posts on their new maps, and the Ministry of Health implemented the National Health Service Act in

In pursuit of morphia

History

regard to mountain rescue, agreeing to supply all drugs and equipment, such as blankets and stretchers, through the Manchester Royal Infirmary.

As Hey's professional home, this hospital was instrumental in the supply of morphia to the posts, providing an interface between mountain rescue and the Ministry of Health and the Welsh Office and, later, the Department of Health and Social Security. The procedure for issue remained in place for many years. Nowadays, mountain rescue teams are issued with morphia by their local medical practitioners on the understanding that complete records are kept, detailing the quantity, batch number and 'use by' date.

Meanwhile, the press turned their attention to the growing toll of mountain accidents. The end of the second world war had brought a massive increase in outdoor activity. But, as the Manchester Guardian complained in the summer of 1948, 'our hills are swarming with town bred youngsters who have no idea how quickly and inevitably their untrained muscles and ill-clad bodies would succumb to exhaustion and exposure if they were trapped for the night without shelter in a blizzard or a freezing mist. For the most part they do not venture on rock climbs but they will blithely run the greater risks of scrambling on steep dry grass in plain leather soles or glissading down a slope of soft snow into a sunless gully, where they find themselves out of control on a sheet of ice.'

By 1950, the First Aid Committee of Mountaineering Clubs had become the Mountain Rescue Committee, a charitable trust with membership from a far wider spectrum of outdoor pursuit groups such as the Youth Hostel Association, the Ramblers Association and many University Clubs.

Mountain rescue continued to be delivered on an ad hoc basis, according to need, until events in Coniston and Keswick prompted the formation of the first civilian teams, led and inspired by remarkable men. Similar stirrings were occurring in the mountains of Scotland and North Wales – where the RAF mountain rescue service, initially conceived for the rescue of crew downed in the mountains, was becoming increasingly involved in the rescue of civilians. And, as the leading figures in mountain rescue travelled from the Lakes to Snowdon, from the Peak District to the Yorkshire Dales, and across the Highlands, in search of new climbs to master, doubtless ideas were exchanged.

In pursuit of morphia

History

CONISTON FELLS RESCUE
PARTY c1947

Coniston and Keswick take the lead

Tourism had begun to intrude into Coniston following the opening of the railway in 1859 and the launching of the lake steamer 'Gondola' that same year. As was often the way, the local folk rarely made a habit of walking the fells but rock climbers began to visit Wasdale during the 1880s, testing their mettle on Dow Crags, at the southern end of the Wetherlam, or Coniston Old Man ridge, en route from the railway station to Wasdale Head. Should any fall, their transport from the hill was likely to be via horse and flat cart until Billy Fury, local carrier, coal merchant and landlord of the Black Bull Hotel, bought a lorry. Volunteers were collected from the bridge by the church in the centre of the village or from the pubs, and the stretcher would be borrowed from the lean-to shed at the back of the Institute, where the village fire engine was garaged. There was no protective clothing. Rescuers simply went up the hill wearing the clothes in which they stood.

Transport to the hospital, once the casualty had been brought down, depended on what was available at the time. Jack Hellen, whose parents owned the local garage, recalled a rescue in 1932 when the patient, a young lady with a fractured femur from a climbing accident on Dow Crag, was conveyed to a nursing home in Ulverston in the back of a seven seater saloon, a Crossley owned by the garage. He also recalled the day Dr Buchanan set a quarryman's fractured tibia and fibula at the foot of Hodge Close quarry without the benefit of xray or anaesthetic. 'My, it did make him sweat and turn red but he didn't shout out!'

The Coniston Fells Rescue Party was formed when a walker from a local guest house triggered a mountain search extending over several days of the vilest weather. Newly married Ernest John Harris Sivyer and his wife Mary arrived at the Holiday Fellowship Centre at Monk Coniston Hall, where Eric was to take up the post of secretary and guide. The morning of 20 December 1946 dawned cold and frosty as they stepped from the train, having travelled through the night.

Later that same morning, forty one year old Eric, having breakfasted and settled in to the accommodation, set off across the fells to familiarise himself with the area. By evening, he had not returned and the police were called. At first light the next day, a rapidly assembled party of local people – including mountain guide Jim Cameron – set out to search the area around Dow Crags and Coniston Old Man to no avail.

By next morning, fifty policemen – drafted in from far afield – had joined farmers and other willing volunteers to search over 100 square miles of countryside in the most appalling conditions. Heavy rain in the valley turned to snow higher up, with mist down to 500 feet and a gale blowing.

As a tiny township at the very top left hand corner of the sprawling county of Lancashire – a county measuring 75 miles in length by 30 miles wide – it was the Lancashire Constabulary who were obliged to deal with any incidents on the local fells. When called upon, police officers might have travelled from the other end of the county and were anything but 'local'.

On 23 December, a young police inspector Tom Andrews made an entry in his personal diary, '5.30am to 6.30pm. Went to Coniston to search for a missing climber.' Late the previous evening, he had been instructed to report to police headquarters in Preston, in uniform, to take charge of a detachment of thirty constables detailed to go to Coniston. At 5.30am they set off, in full uniform, many wearing great coats and macintoshes, caps or helmets and ordinary regulation boots – and some carrying capes.

The previous day, a police detachment from Blackburn had travelled to Coniston led by an inspector from Darwen. It had rained incessantly. Tom recounts the story that the inspector,

Coniston and Keswick take the lead

History

soaked to the skin, asked the wife of the village constable, Jim Leak – who was still out on the fells – if he could come into the police station and have a bath.

'Mrs Leak, a friendly lady and typical of the traditional British village bobby's wife, agreed. Then the inspector asked if there was a chance of his borrowing a set of PC Leak's underwear before putting on his wet uniform. Mrs Leak agreed and, after a hot drink, the inspector returned to Blackburn with his colleagues.' Constable Leak, who had remained on duty until the detachment left, eventually returned home to the police station and had a bath. When finished, he called to his wife 'Mam, I can't find my clean underpants and vest!' His wife replied that she had let the inspector borrow them and PC Leak would have to wait another day. History does not record whether his underpants ever made it back to their rightful owner.

Tasked to lead various groups of searchers, including the police officers, was professional mountain guide Jim Cameron – who himself spent two days checking every gully and ledge where a body might be concealed. He decided they should search Wetherlam and off they set with strict instructions not to lose sight of each other in the mist because, as Jim remarked, 'it wouldn't do to lose a policeman.' However, by the time they reached the summit, there had already been several mishaps. So Jim decided to call off the search and they descended to Coniston and the comfort of a hot meal, courtesy of the mobile police canteen.

By the following day, the RAF had joined the search around Coniston Old Man. With the weather now fairly calm and sunny, Jim set off again to Wetherlam but, as the party made their way to Tilberthwaite, word reached them the casualty had been found at the foot of a waterfall known locally as the White Lady. Sivyer's body was just 500 foot from the main road, where he appeared to have fallen about 400 foot down a steep gully, having perhaps lost his footing scrambling over the ice. Robert Birkett, a farmer from Low Yewdale, had spoken to a man answering Mr Sivyer's description on the Friday.

When interviewed by a Daily Dispatch reporter Birkett said, 'The man asked me if he was trespassing, and then said he was crossing my land because he was taking a direct route to the mountains. He left me to climb Yewdale Crag, ignoring roads and paths.'

The search had taken such a toll on all those involved that local county councillor, Stanley Baker, proposed the formation of a specialist team. When his proposal was considered by the Parish Council, on 24 January 1947, they were unanimous in their support, but were unable to fund the cost from the council budget. So Mr

Coniston and Keswick take the lead

History

Baker called a public meeting, attended by a large number of villagers.

The outcome was a dedicated team of volunteers – the first civilian mountain rescue team in England – led by Jim Cameron. Their first official rescue was on Sunday, 13 April, 1947 when Cameron himself was injured in an accident whilst guiding clients on Dow Crag. Unable to attend the inaugural meeting due to working commitments, he had told colleagues he would be happy to take any job on the committee and was duly elected leader in his absence.

Belayed at the top of a 70 foot pitch on a climb called 'Necklace', the client he was bringing up fell, pulling Jim off his stance. The rope between him and the belay broke and he was hurled to the foot of the crag, where he lay unconscious. One of the party ran down to Torver to raise the alarm and his newly organised team mates made good time to Dow Crag. Jim was carried down by stretcher to George Usher's builder's lorry, parked a short way along the Walna Scar road, which took the stretcher and rescuers back to the village. From there, Jim was taken to Westmorland County Hospital, Kendal where he was found to have sustained nothing more than a broken ankle. Two months later he was back climbing on Dow and continued to lead the team for many years.

Coniston and Keswick take the lead

History

In those early days, team equipment was basic – one stretcher, one hurricane lamp, three ex-army blankets, two climbing ropes and several hot water bottles.

Further north, across the fells in Keswick, a similar story was unfolding, but it was an accident on Great Gable – prompting a local farmer's wife to remark, 'Aye, it's far less trouble when they kill thersels' – which set the scene for a permanent, organised rescue team. On a cold and blustery day, in late April 1946, two experienced climbers had been tackling a climb called Shark's Fin when a gust of wind blew one of the men from his sloping hold. He fell onto a ledge, his femur broken. Back at the Scafell Hotel, his companion enlisted the help of two more climbers and, armed with medical supplies, a stretcher and food, they set off to the scene of the accident. On the way, they met with Horace 'Rusty' Westmorland, a local climber recently returned to Cumbria from thirty six years living, working and climbing in Canada. Rusty and a young companion had been on their homeward journey, having opted for a less challenging route than first intended due to the poor weather, when they were met by the youths. Rusty climbed a gully to the left of Hell's Gate, to the top of Needle Ridge, then down the top two pitches of Tophet Bastion and looked down the Shark's Fin, where he could see

Wilfred Noyce on an exposed ledge, secured by a rope belayed to a spike nearly forty feet above. Rusty climbed down to the injured man and did what he could to make him more comfortable.

Arrangements had been made with the police for a follow up party to assist in the evacuation of the casualty and to provide food, blankets, torches and other necessary equipment. A stretcher party of six made their way onto the crag and down to Noyce. By 7pm he was wrapped in a down bag and blankets and strapped to a stretcher with his leg splinted. The rescuers did not have sufficient rope to barrowboy 200 foot down the climb so it was decided to haul the stretcher to the top of the crag about 120 foot above. Two ropes were fastened to the stretcher head and one man to each rope climbed 20 or 30 foot, found a suitable belay, took in the slack rope and snubbed the stretcher to prevent it falling back. The remaining four men held on to the stretcher side bars, gained footholds and, when given the word, heaved the stretcher up a few inches. Slack was taken in and the procedure repeated.

Casualty and stretcher were literally inched up the crag. It took three and a half painful hours, in mist and heavy rain interspersed with wet snow, to reach the top. During this time, voices had been heard sweeping up the crags so it was assumed a relief party was on the way. The

Coniston and Keswick take the lead

History

BORROWDALE ST JOHN AMBULANCE
BRIGADE 1929

131

EARLY KESWICK
MOUNTAIN RESCUERS

rescuers expected that, once the crag had been scaled and the casualty lowered down the gully into Hell's Gate, there would be a fresh party of men to relieve them. But as darkness fell, and with 1500 foot of scree to negotiate before the Styhead track, it became apparent that the support party, unable to hear any response to their calls, had returned to base taking with them precious torches, food and hot drinks.

There followed a laborious lower down the scree where the rescue party were in constant danger of falling rocks, dislodged by the anchor men who, having paid out all their rope, had to negotiate the scree in darkness groping for fresh belays. Meanwhile Noyce had refused the morphia which may have relieved his suffering.

As daylight dawned, the exhausted rescue party was met by two policemen from Wasdale Head and an RAF mountain rescue team which had been standing by with a jeep to ferry the casualty to a waiting ambulance. It had been twenty one hours, much of it endured without food, in foul weather and darkness.

Concerned at the lack of any joined up rescue service, and the apparent ease with which the relief party organised by the police had given up the search and returned to base leaving neither men, light, nor sustenance, Rusty decided to do something positive. While the police, acting as crown agents, would take possession of a

Coniston and
Keswick take
the lead

History

deceased body, they were not obliged to help injured walkers or climbers, let alone being trained or equipped to do so. In the summer of that year, he appealed through a local newspaper for volunteers to form a mountain rescue team and had 34 replies, four from local doctors. However, as quickly as the number of volunteers grew, so the odd few would drop out. Undeterred, he pressed on.

A letter in the Keswick Reminder in November 1947 asked for more names of 'willing climbers, fell walkers, young shepherds, young quarrymen and others.' For anyone concerned about loss of earnings during a rescue, a reimbursement of up to £1 was available from national sources which later would be claimed from the rescued individual or their family or friends – although, in the event, no such claim was ever made.

By April 1948, some thirty men had volunteered and, with Rusty as leader, the Borrowdale MRT had their first official call out when a dozen members helped police, shepherds, farmers and other volunteers in a search for a twenty seven year old walker on Cross Fell, who had been missing for three days. Deep snow and strong winds hampered the search and it was some time later before the body was found by a group of boy ramblers on the Alston side of the fell.

The story echoed across the UK, as a variety of accidents, searches and light aircraft crashes in mountainous and moorland areas galvanised the locals into action. Initially, there was little direct communication between teams in different regions, the only common thread the six monthly meetings of the Mountain Rescue Committee at Hey's rooms in St John Street, Manchester. And yet, new teams continued to spring up with similar values, similar aspirations, each subtly adapted to their own environment. The inspiration to set up a team might come from anywhere – the local police officer, GP, hotelier or mountaineering enthusiast. Anyone, in fact, who saw a need for specialised assistance in first aid and search capability.

Whereas today's national body is made up of representatives of the eight regional bodies – the Lakes, Mid Pennines, North East, North Wales, Peak District, South Wales, South West England and the Yorkshire Dales – then it was the individual teams who would apply for affiliation to the Mountain Rescue Committee. Through the 50s and 60s, almost every meeting saw new applications to affiliate although, in many cases, these were not acceptable due to insufficient experience or geographical location but might be categorised as 'recognised teams'.

An affiliated body was expected to fulfil certain criteria – it should be reasonably permanent and

Coniston and
Keswick take
the lead

History

well organised, with proper equipment for its job, under experienced leadership and with satisfactory arrangements in place for being summoned when needed – and a report must be sent on all accidents, not only for record purposes, but also to satisfy the requirements of the insurance policy and the regulations governing the issue of morphia. A further requirement was that rescue kits be made available for moorland and mountain accidents as well as caving mishaps and the police fully informed of this.

The importance of education

In the Lake District, Outward Bound schools at Eskdale and Ullswater began teaching mountain rescue as part of their courses. In fact, education was a significant factor in the development of mountain rescue, as the popularity of climbing and the incidence of accidents continued to grow, and with it the demand for more formal training in outdoor skills. By the late 1950s, several education authorities were seeking to establish their own outdoor activity centres. Plas y Brenin, ideally placed at the heart of Snowdonia, was such an example. By 1960, the centre was a designated post and basic mountain rescue courses had been included in the programme. Students would regularly help out with stretcher carries and searches. Involvement was purely voluntary but each incident represented a huge commitment in time and effort for those in the rescue parties who already spent their professional lives out on the hill as instructors and guides, and would often turn up to work straight from a rescue or turn out on a rescue after a hard day's work.

The main rescue centre for North Wales had initially been Idwal Cottage. Constance Alexander and Olive Pritchard, wardens at this climbing hostel, were both very active rescuers. The emphasis moved to Ogwen Cottage when the Climbing Club moved the rescue kit there and Mr Hughes, son in law of Mrs Williams of Ogwen Cottage, began to help by using his taxi as rescue transport. In 1959, climbers Ron James and Tony Mason-Hornby bought the Cottage and opened the first permanent private mountaineering school. It's said that Mrs Williams' parting words of advice on rescue were, 'Fire a red flare from the car park – get the climbers together and put the one with the cleanest boots in charge.'

The importance of education

History

Ogwen Cottage was very quickly recognised as an active mountain rescue post, the instructors automatically became members of the Ogwen Cottage rescue team, available for call out at any time. As the centre was opened throughout the year, there was always a core of competent mountaineers available and, for the next five years, aided and advised by Flight Sergeant Johnnie Lees, leader of the RAF Valley MRT, the fledgling team carried out many rescues in their own area and assisted their neighbours on Snowdon.

The synergy between mountain rescue and education was also apparent in Scotland. Glenmore Lodge had opened its doors as Scotland's National Outdoor Training Centre in 1947, with the Reverend Canon Bob Clarke as its warden. Previously the Episcopalian Minister in Fort William and a founder member of the Lochaber team, he boasted considerable mountaineering experience. As in Wales, staff and students at Glenmore would so routinely become involved in rescue operations simply due to their presence on the hill, that agreement to participate in mountain rescue was written into the job description. Since its establishment, the Lodge has continued to deliver mountain training to thousands of team members.

The RAF
play a key part

The involvement of Johnnie Lees in the development of mountain rescue in North Wales represented the major influence of the RAF on the service in general. RAF teams played a big part in the early growth and evolution of several civilian teams, essentially through the provision of equipment and training expertise. Flt Lt George Graham at Llandwrog and Flt Lt David Crichton at Harpur Hill have been acknowledged as probably the first mountain rescue team as we would recognise it today. These men were putting together scratch teams to rescue crashed airmen in the mountains from early in the war. Ad hoc teams were rallied by the station tannoy and went to the rescue in their working battledress, rubber boots and RAF greatcoats, accompanied by the station medical officer with his little black bag and a basic boy scout compass.

Throughout 1943, despite the best efforts of the rescue teams, as many as 571 aircrew had lost their lives in 220 crashes across the UK. It was clear there was a need for a more structured service. At Llandwrog, an instructional army team delivered two weeks intensive training in navigation, rock climbing and hill walking. The ground was laid for a service capable of responding beyond its original focus and, the following summer, the Llandwrog team were called to assist their first civilian climber, a young girl who had become stranded on Cader Idris. In the event, she had been found safe and well, having made her own way down without help.

The Air Ministry was keen to encourage the assistance of RAF teams in civilian climbing incidents as these operations presented the ideal opportunity to develop skills, self–reliance and initiative. From the civilian point of view, the RAF could provide manpower, specialist equipment and good radio communications. And they were always available, no matter what day of the week or hour of the day. That spirit of teamwork and collaboration continues to this day, as RAF helicopter squadrons spend 95% of their time working on civilian operations.

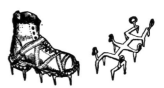

CRAMPON FITTED TO
BOOT WITH LANIERE

It was Black Easter, in 1951, when events conspired to move the cause of mountain rescue further forward. It had been a long, wet winter, with a great deal of snow on high ground and little sign of respite for the first walking weekend of the year. The British Mountaineering Council reported that 'continued snowfall meant unusual cornices and dangerous ice slopes which ordinary fell walkers were unable to cope with. Even with ice axes, some of the slopes, quite safe under normal conditions, had become very dangerous'.

By the end of the Easter weekend, nine people had lost their lives on Snowdon and a further five would die before the year was out. There was a public outcry, fuelled by the press, with calls for restricted access to Snowdon without much thought as to how that might be effected. It was suggested that scouts be appointed who could report on conditions on the mountains and issue warnings through the media. Less than a year later, the National Park wardens were doing that very thing and thoughts were crystallising about how an efficient mountain rescue service could operate in the area.

The RAF Valley team had played a key part in the events of the weekend, recovering three bodies and four casualties, even lending out their ice axes to one group struggling over an icy stretch on the Snowdon Horseshoe. In Scotland,

The RAF play their part

History

just a week prior to that, an incident on Torridon, when an Avro Lancaster bomber failed to return from a training exercise, proved a turning point for the team at RAF Kinloss.

Besides the huge press interest these incidents generated, they served another purpose. Suddenly Whitehall was listening. The Air Ministry implemented radical changes for the RAF teams – a structured training schedule, the introduction of an annual mountaineering course in North Wales, an instruction book for mountain rescue and the secondment of experienced mountaineers to the RAF MRS.

Scotland breaks away

Through the 50s, Scotland became a focus for a post-war generation of working class youngsters keen to sharpen their skills. New posts were established to meet the demand in the popular climbing areas but, as accidents began to increase, it was clear the fragmented development and uncoordinated nature of Scottish mountain rescue was far from satisfactory. In April 1960, two meetings were held in Perth under the chairmanship of Dr Donald Duff of the Cairngorm Club.

The result was a consultative council, set up to foster education through suitable publicity and help with the formation and training of rescue teams and the siting and supervision of equipment. A Scottish subcommittee, initially led by Duff (succeeded by Colonel Jack Arthur of the Red Cross), would work in conjunction with the MRC to deal with day to day problems. It was the first step towards a separate Scottish mountain rescue service.

By the following year, the investigating committee appointed to draw up a constitution and method of working for the new subcommittee had recommended the retention of both the Scottish Council and the Scottish Subcommittee but with full powers to the subcommittee, which would change its name to the Scottish Branch of the MRC.

By 1962, it was proposed that any future subscriptions received from the Scottish clubs go direct to the Scottish Branch, although the committee disagreed. However, this was a suggestion which would not go away.

By the end of November 1964 there was a proposal from the Scottish Mountaineering Club that the Scottish Branch be extended to include representatives from nine of the main Scottish voluntary teams, including Glenmore Lodge, as

Scotland
breaks away

History

well as RAF Leuchars and Kinloss and the chief constables of Argyll, Inverness-shire, North East counties and Ross-shire, which would meet twice a year at Fort William. The aim of this extended Scottish subcommittee would be to look at matters peculiar to the Scottish mountains and Scottish mountain rescue, such as the special problems presented by skiing accidents. It made sense.

A draft constitution, presented to the MRC by Jack Arthur, was agreed after much discussion and, in June 1965, in the Red Cross rooms in Bath Street, Glasgow, the Mountain Rescue Committee of Scotland was formed. Together with sister organisations in Ireland and Northern Ireland, the MRC of Scotland continue to maintain close links with Mountain Rescue in England and Wales and co-operate in their joint objectives.

Meanwhile, teams continued to emerge and grow, and even merge and grow, through the seventies, eighties and nineties and into the new millennium. The Mountain Rescue Council for England and Wales now operates as 'Mountain Rescue England and Wales' and boasts fifty nine teams in England and Wales including cave rescue and RAF teams, with over three thousand volunteer members.

Over the years, the growth in mountain rescue teams took its toll on the old rescue post system which has now all but disappeared. With the exception of organised groups such as the National Park Rangers, who continue to use the odd post, most of the remaining posts are either in isolated climbing areas or those used by local teams as equipment dumps, located where they see fit. Almost all are now fully secured, as vandalism and theft previously left many without equipment when it was most needed. In 1989, Ordnance Survey was asked to reverse the previous landmark decision to show rescue posts on maps of England and Wales. They were also omitted from the official Mountain Rescue Handbook from 1992 and, in November 1993, the MRC took the decision not to supply mountain rescue posts in the future.

Scotland
breaks away

History

145

A work in progress

From the start, mountain rescuers have been a creative bunch – and that spirit of research, development and innovation in the cause of better casualty care has continued.

Since the development of the Thomas stretcher, the first designed specifically for mountain use, the search for the 'perfect' mountain stretcher has continued to drive a dedicated few. In the fifties and sixties, the Duff stretcher, designed by Donald Duff, was popular. It was a simple steel tubular frame, with no handles and channelled steel runners extended along two thirds of its length. For transport to an incident, the runners could be detached and the remainder folded in two for carriage in a backpack. A wheel could also be added. Weighing about 30lbs, the Duff stretcher formed part of the equipment inventory for the successful British expedition to Everest in 1953.

By the seventies Hamish McInnes, in Scotland, and Peter Bell, in the Lake District, had taken up the baton. And more recently, the MRC of Scotland has set about producing a new generation of mountain stretcher. Stretchers provide stability and safety for the casualty and enable rescuers to carry an injured person

A work in progress

History

LANGDALE AMBLESIDE MRT
Photo: Ashley Cooper Photography

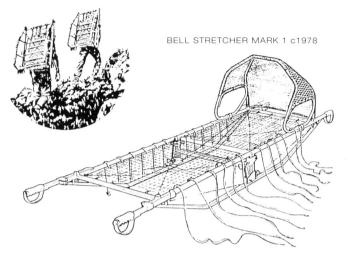

across uneven terrain for long distances. They also provide a safe way to winch someone into a hovering helicopter, although helicopters are only permitted to winch stretchers that have met MOD requirements.

The Bell stretcher has been the mainstay for teams in England and Wales for over thirty five years and established a reputation for toughness and rugged durability in the most demanding of situations – although some teams also continue to use the original Thomas. Essentially, teams will employ whichever stretcher they feel is best suited to their own terrain, their preferred techniques and their members' strengths, abilities and, of course, the circumstances of the particular incident.

Other equipment developed and adopted

specifically with the mountain casualty in mind includes the casualty bag, the vacuum mattress and warm air breathing apparatus. The modern casbag encapsulates the casualty, complete with any splinting, whilst allowing access to rescuers to continue monitoring the comfort and medical state of the casualty during transit. The vacuum mattress is, effectively, a full body immobilisation and can even remain in place during any subsequent x-ray treatment. The warm air breather allows the treatment of hypothermia by producing warm air for the patient to inhale.

One of the greatest developments of the last seventy five years has been in radio communications. A spate of air crashes in the early forties prompted the RAF to review the problems caused by the complete absence of communication between search party members. Fl Lt Graham, at Llandwrog in North Wales, subsequently introduced the idea of portable wireless sets. These had been in use by the army for some time but nobody had thought of using them in mountain rescue work.

The idea was that an ambulance fitted with wireless could contact both the portable sets and the wireless set of the parent station. The wireless set in the ambulance had a long range and a short range transmission. The long range was used for messages between the parent

A work in progress

History

station and the ambulance at mountain HQ, the short range for messages between mountain HQ and members of the search party carrying the portable wireless sets.

Police forces also had access to portable wireless, although for the early civilian rescue teams fortunate enough to make use of the police radio facility, this generally came strapped to a police officer and weighed heavily. By contrast, the majority of team members today carry their own two-way radio tucked in the top of their rucksack, a speaker/microphone facility attached to a shoulder strap. Team vehicles, mobile control units and team headquarters are also fully equipped with radios, so communications between all the personnel involved can be maintained through every stage of an incident.

Satellite and mobile phone technology have also hugely advanced the communications capability of mountain rescue teams and their casualties. It's hard to imagine that once there was rarely even a phone line at the foot of a mountain or in the local hotel. A regular feature of committee minutes was the request for a telephone box to be established near a post or the use of the local hotel telephone line to be agreed and, where no such facility existed, the use of AA and RAC boxes might be arranged.

Where once a team was rallied by whatever

means was possible – be it letter, newspaper announcement or one man on a bicycle touring the village to rally support – pagers have been the preferred means of alert over the last twenty years. However, these are now fast losing ground to the mobile phone text message.

The use of mobile phones to report incidents on the mountains has increased exponentially over the last ten years. Sometimes these calls are avoidable but the majority are warranted and lives are saved. Often the caller can provide sufficient information to the rescue team to speed their arrival at the casualty site and liaise with the appropriate emergency services to effect a rapid evacuation from the hill.

The downside to this growing dependency on the mobile is that, whilst they work very well within urban areas, coverage is often limited in mountainous areas and varies between networks.

GPS technology has enabled casualties to provide rescue teams with their exact location and, thanks to further developments, teams are now beginning to be able to plot their movements and position on a map in real time.

The medical treatment of casualties has also improved considerably. The early ad hoc rescue parties invariably counted a local doctor or two in their number but their colleagues would have been largely unskilled and untrained in medical

A work in
progress

History

procedures or casualty care. Most teams now have a medical officer, usually a doctor or other medical professional, who will guide the members in best practice, but there are also likely to be a number of members who are nurses or paramedics in their day jobs. In recent years, the MRC has introduced a basic standard which all mountain rescue members are expected to achieve – specifically the ability to perform a basic primary survey into the airway, breathing and circulation of the casualty and carry out potentially life saving procedures. A comprehensive Casualty Care Course has been devised and the majority of team members undergo this rigorous training and assessment in order to achieve the MRC Casualty Care Certificate. Many team members continue to develop their skills through more advanced first aid training. The aim now is as it was seventy five years ago – to improve the comfort, safety and well being of the casualty. To save lives.

So much has changed and yet one essential thing has remained the same. Mountain rescue continues to be fiercely protective of its voluntary ethic, team members providing their service free of charge to those unfortunate enough to need our help. Of course, there is a real cost in terms of the medical equipment, stretchers, vehicles and fuel, radios and communications, ropes and climbing hardware, insurances and maintenance of team bases, and teams rely on the generosity of the general public, donations and legacies to provide the wherewithal for these. And behind every team are the many costs met by the team members themselves, from providing their own protective clothing and equipment and often travelling many miles in their own vehicle to respond to an incident, to the phone calls, postage and admin costs of running the team. And not to mention ever increasing demands on their time.

So please do give generously next time you see a team's collection box on the bar.

© Judy Whiteside

Sources

Mountain Rescue Council archives
Call Out. The First 50 Years by George Bott
A Short History of Lakeland Climbing Part 1 by H M Kelly & J H Doughty
A Perilous Playground by Bob Maslen–Jones
The Technique of Mountaineering by J E B Wright
A History of Scottish Mountain Rescue by Mountain Rescue Committee of Scotland
www.rucksackclub.org
www.rescuestretchers.co.uk
Mountain Rescue by Bob Sharp & Judy Whiteside

With thanks also to David Allan, Tom Andrew, Dr James Armstrong, Roy Cooksey, Bob Henson, Paul Horder, Bob Sharp.

Access & conservation

www.naturalengland.org.uk
Natural England for everything about access
and conservation in England including advice,
maps and guides, grants and funding.
www.ccw.gov.uk
The Countryside Council for Wales.
www.outdooraccess-scotland.com
The Scottish Outdoor Access Code.
www.bobw.co.uk
Best of Both Worlds for how outdoor recreation
and conservation can go hand in hand.

Weather

www.metoffice.gov.uk
The Met Office.
www.mwis.org.uk
The Mountain Weather Information Service.
www.sais.gov.uk
Sportscotland Avalanche Information Service.
www.lake-district.gov.uk/weatherline
5 day forecast for the Lake District.
**www.scottishsport.co.uk/walking/
avalanche.htm**
Avalanche info.
www.midgeforecast.co.uk
Seasonal forecast on the midge count in 38
areas of Scotland.

National Parks

Broads Authority
www.broads-authority.gov.uk
Brecon Beacons National Park
www.breconbeacons.org
Dartmoor National Park
www.dartmoor-npa.gov.uk
Exmoor National Park
www.exmoor-nationalpark.gov.uk
The New Forest
www.thenewforest.co.uk
Lake District National Park
www.lake-district.gov.uk

Northumberland National Park
www.nnpa.org.uk
North York Moors National Park
www.visitnorthyorkmoors.org.uk
Peak District National Park
www.peakdistrict.org
Pembrokeshire Coast National Park
www.pcnpa.org.uk
Snowdonia National Park
www.eryri-npa.gov.uk
Yorkshire Dales National Park
www.yorkshiredales.org.uk
Cairngorms National Park Authority
www.cairngorms.co.uk
Lock Lomond and The Trossachs National Park
www.lochlomond-trossachs.org

Useful organisations

British Mountaineering Council
Training, guidebooks and DVDs, clubs and huts, equipment advice and insurance and member services including 'Summit' magazine.
177-179 Burton Rd, Manchester M20 2BB
T: 0161 445 6111 **www.thebmc.co.uk**

Mountaineering Council of Scotland
Mountain safety, climbing competitions, mountaineering and climbing ethics, codes of practice, insurance and members services including 'The Scottish Mountaineer' magazine.
The Old Granary, West Mill Street, Perth PH1 5QP
T: 01738 493942 **www.mcofs.org.uk**

Mountain Leader Training UK
Training and assessment for leaders, instructors and guides including books, videos and DVDs.
MLTUK, Siabod Cottage, Capel Curig, Conwy LL24 0ES
T: 01690 720272 **www.mltuk.org**

Association of Mountaineering Intructors
Find a qualified mountaineering instructor.
AMI, Siabod Cottage, Capel Curig, Conwy
LL24 0ES
T: 01690 720123 **www.ami.org.uk**

British Caving Association
The Old Methodist Chapel, Great Hucklow,
Buxton, Derbyshire SK17 8RG
www.british-caving.org.uk

Useful publications to learn and hone your skills

Mountaincraft and Leadership by Eric
Langmuir. Published jointly by Mountain
Leader Training England (MLTE) and Mountain
Leader Training Scotland (MLTS). First
published as 'Mountain Leadership' 1969.
ISBN: 9781850602958.

Mountain Navigation by Peter Cliff.
Published by Menasha Ridge Press.
ISBN: 9781871890556.

Hill Walking by Steve Long. The official
handbook of the Mountain Leader and
Walking Group Leader schemes. Essential
reference for anybody undertaking these
schemes. ISBN: 9780954151102.

Rock Climbing by Libby Peter. Published by
MLTUK. Essential skills and techniques for rock
climbing. ISBN: 9780954151119.

**The International Handbook of Technical
Mountaineering** by Pete Hill. Published by
David & Charles plc. A comprehensive guide
to a wide range of mountaineering techniques
in A–Z format. ISBN: 9780715321669.

**The Ultimate Hillwalking Skills
Handbook** by Chris Bagshaw. Published by
David & Charles plc. ISBN: 9780715322543.

Mountain Weather. Understanding Britain's Mountain Weather by David Pedgley. Published by Cicerone. ISBN: 9781852844806.

Pocket First Aid and Wilderness Medicine by Jim Duff and Peter Gormly. Published by Cicerone. ISBN: 9781852845001.

Navigation. Using Your Map and Compass by Pete Hawkins. Published by Cicerone. ISBN: 9781852844905.

Map and Compass. The Art of Navigation by Pete Hawkins. Published by Cicerone. ISBN: 9781852843946.

Snow. Understanding, Testing and Interpreting Snow Conditions to Make Better Avalanche Predictions by Robert Bolognesi. Published by Cicerone. ISBN: 9781852844745.

Avalanche. Understand and Reduce the Risks from Avalanches by Robert Bolognesi. Published by Cicerone. ISBN: 9781852844738.

Winter Skills. Essential Walking and Climbing Techniques by Andy Cunningham and Allen Fyffe. Published by MLTUK. The official handbook for the Mountaineering Instructor (MIC) and Winter Mountain Leader (WML) schemes. ISBN: 9780954151133.

Casualty Care in Mountain Rescue edited by John Ellerton. Published by Mountain Rescue England and Wales. ISBN: 9780950176574.

reference

To find out more about mountain and cave rescue

Mountain Rescue by Bob Sharp and Judy Whiteside. Published by Hayloft Publishing. Everything you ever wanted to ask about mountain rescue together with real life stories from the rescuers and the rescued.
ISBN: 9781904524397.

So You Want to Join Mountain Rescue? by David Allan and Judy Whiteside. Published by Hayloft Publishing. A light hearted look at the world of mountain rescue told in cartoons.
ISBN: 9781904524472.

Mountain Rescue. History and Development in the Peak District by Ian Hurst and Roger Bennett. Published by Tempus Publishing Ltd.
ISBN: 9780752440910.

999... Mountain Rescue Please by Paul Hitchen. A lighthearted view of 50 years of rescues by Glossop MRT.
ISBN: 9780955137716.

The Team by Sheila Richardson. The story of Cockermouth MRT. ISBN 10: 09526 6657X.

Call Out. The First 50 Years by George Bott. The story of Keswick MRT.
ISBN 10: 0953109801.

Chance in a Million by Bob Barton and Blyth Wright. Published by Scottish Mountaineering Trust. ISBN: 9780907521594.

It's Only a Game! by Jim Eyre.
Published by Wild Places Publishing.
ISBN: 9780952670162.

The Game Goes On by Jim Eyre.
Published by Wild Places Publishing.
ISBN: 9780952670179.

Cave Exploring The Definitive Guide to Caving by Jill Florio. Published by Falcon Guides. ISBN: 9780762725601.

The Complete Caving Manual by Andy Sparrow. Published by The Crowood Press Ltd. ISBN: 9781847971463.

To support mountain rescue

Basecamp
Support all mountain rescue teams in England and Wales by joining Basecamp. £24 per year for single and £42 for joint membership, includes subscription to 'Mountain Rescue' magazine.
Basecamp, White Cottage, 9 Main Road, Grindleford, Hope Valley Derbyshire S32 1JN.

National Fundraising
For information on sponsorship, fundraising opportunities or Basecamp details, contact nationalfundraising@mountain.rescue.org.uk

Mountain Rescue England and Wales
Give online at www.mountain.rescue.org.uk

National Press Officer
T: 0870 240 4024 9.00am to 5.00pm. Please note this is NOT an emergency number. If you require mountain rescue, dial 999 and ask for the police.

Acknowledgments

Thanks to all those who have provided gems of insight, supplied information, given permission for use of their photography or illustrations (as credited individually) or helped out on the proof reading. Special thanks and acknowledgment to:

David Allan, Peter Bell, John Coombs, Coniston MRT, John Ellerton, Dave Freeborn, Mick Guy, Bob Henson, Paul Horder, Keswick MRT, Mike Margeson, Tick Alert, MLTUK, Resuscitation Council (UK), Barry Robinson, Bob Sharp, Andy Simpson.

reference

personal notes

index

About the author: Judy Whiteside didn't so much join mountain rescue as find herself slowly but relentlessly sucked deeper into it, in the manner of quicksand. She has been involved at local and national level for the past twelve years, the last ten as editor of Mountain Rescue Magazine.

In the intervening years, though not an operational team member, she has undergone full team member training, sat the cascare exams, soaked up the history, attended incidents, spent seven years as her local team secretary, organised events, and written and illustrated a number of articles and books on all things mountain rescue, as well as meeting and exchanging ideas and opinions with mountain rescue personnel across the UK.

In her day job she is a freelance designer, writer and illustrator but, given the opportunity to escape the computer screen, will invariably head for the hills, walking boots and waterproofs at the ready!

Mountains and moorlands can be treacherous places without proper care. Of course, there's no substitute for experience but there are steps you can take to minimise the chances of getting hurt or lost.

Quite frankly, we'd rather you didn't become just another mountain rescue statistic! But what if you do become involved in an accident? What if you meet an avalanche or a thunderstorm threatens? How do you call out mountain rescue and what can you do as you await their arrival? You hold the answers in your hands.

New for this second edition is the first aid section, packed with valuable advice for you and the casualty.

So pack us in your rucksack, take to the hills and enjoy!

Mountain Rescue England and Wales
in association with
British Cave Rescue